# RESULTS FASTER!

## TONY JEARY

Clovercroft Publishing

RESULTS Faster!

©2016 by Tony Jeary

Published by Clovercroft Publishing, Franklin, Tennessee.

Published in association with Larry Carpenter of Christian Book Services, LLC.
www.christianbookservices.com

Cover Design by Brooke Hawkins

Interior Design by Suzanne Lawing

Edited by Adept Content Solutions

Printed in the United States of America

978-1-945507-18-2

# CONTENTS

**Thinking**: Change your thinking, change your results.

**Beliefs**: Be sure the principles on your *Belief Window* are true, accurate, and current—not outdated, not off mark, and not false.

**Strategic IQ**: Not only balance tactical and strategic, but also be *Intentionally Strategic* about everything if you want the right results faster.

**Wealth**: We all want it, and it's a lot more than money. It's living on purpose and spending time doing what makes you happy and/or what you're really passionate about.

**Values**: Whether it's business or just you, a must have are clearly defined values that align with your goals and vision for the future.

**Goal Setting**: Goals need to be written, visualized, and mentally owned, and then you can actually Design Your Own Life.

**MOLO**: Know what you want more of, know what you want less of, know what you should do more of, and know what you should do less of.

**HLAs**: Clearly defined HLAs are the secret to avoiding distractions and multiplying achievement, both personally and professionally.

**Saying "No"**: Saying "No" smartly pays huge rewards!

**Time**: Where and how you invest your time and energy will determine your results! Period!

**Presentation Mastery™**: Life truly is a series of presentations.

**Strategic Selling**: Being strategic versus just being skillful can greatly impact the results you get.

# INTRODUCTION

We deal with results in every phase of our lives. We're graded for results in school. We compete for results in business. Every day we measure vast amounts of data to get better understanding and better results. Results are a key indicator of the choices we make in our lives and our effectiveness in executing those choices.

Consider your own life and business for a moment. What results you are getting? Are they the results you want? Most people want better results, and they want them faster. In fact, taking their vision to reality in less time is what I help others do, virtually every day of my life.

So, welcome to *RESULTS Faster!* We're embarking on an exciting journey together to discover how to not only get better results, but to get them at a strategically accelerated rate. This book and its complementary online course are a compilation under a single title of the best of my life's work, including the forty-five plus books I've published and the hundreds of courses I've developed to help people get the results they want and get them faster.

You may have noticed my moniker, The RESULTS Guy™, on the cover of the book. Let me tell you a little about myself, my commitment to encouraging others to produce and be their best, and how that moniker came about. I grew up in an entrepreneurial family, and I parlayed that information and knowledge into a ton of very profitable entrepreneurial ventures. Then the market changed and it all … well … went away. That's when I stepped back and asked, *What do I truly want to do with my life?* As I explored the various possibilities and continued to challenge my own thinking (like I will yours), I knew what I had just been through was going to shape me for the rest of my life. **I realized that I actually wanted to impact people with my experiences and the lessons I had learned, so I started on my life's journey of studying, accumulating, and learning best practices so I could super-charge others.** In 1995 I set out to impact the world with outstanding presentation strategies, and I ended up coaching such high profile clients as the president of the largest company in the world, Walmart, and writing over twenty-five books on the subject of presentation effectiveness. In 2006, though, I recognized that my true dream was about to become a reality. That's the year that Jim Norman, who had been my coach for over a decade, finally agreed to come on board as my company president.

Jim was a special man. He was the former president of Zig Ziglar's corporation; and when he left that position, I asked him to be my president. He wanted to run his own consulting company; he did agree, though, to be my coach. And after ten years of coaching me, shaping my thinking, and seeing my work impact others, and through my continual persistence and persuasion (one of the things I talk about in this book), he finally relented and became my president. That was a major blessing. It was during his tenure with me that we launched my signature book, *Strategic Acceleration.*

At that point Jim said, "Tony, you now have enough track record that you truly can live up to the moniker, 'The Results Guy.'" I was so excited to realize that I was actually living out my life-long dream of impacting people and helping them reach new heights, both personally and professionally, so we officially trademarked the name. Since that time I've doubled down on pulling together all of my best practices, knowledge, and insights and putting them into a format I can share, both in person and in my writings, and now in the video course, to help people get more of the results they want faster, hence the moniker, "The Results Guy™."

**I'VE BEEN HONORED AND BLESSED TO HAVE PEOPLE SEEK ME OUT TO BE THEIR COACH.**

Throughout my career I've been honored and blessed to have people seek me out to be their coach—top achievers, such as the president of Walmart I mentioned earlier, the president of Samsung, the president of Ford, the president of Firestone, the president of TGI Fridays, and even people from the Forbes Richest 400, as well as the Sergeant-at-Arms of the US Senate. When you work with people with that high a profile year after year like I've done now for decades, you're going to pick up distinctions they have proven out that allow you to be even sharper. I basically have a run of over thirty years of helping others, and I've been learning from them the whole way. It's been an interesting journey, and one I'm excited to condense into this book for you.

In my life's work, I've been very fortunate to develop a formula that dramatically impacts the ability of a person, a small team, a large group, or even a whole organization to get more results in an accelerated format. That's how we came up with the title *Strategic Acceleration* for the best-selling book that teaches how to get accelerated results through the formula Clarity, Focus, and Execution. I've also been fortunate to have several other best sellers. One in particular, *Life Is a Series of Presentations,* which was published by Simon and Schuster, was recently recommended by Daymond John from *Shark Tank*. From his perspective, my book ranks right up there with *Think and Grow Rich* and *Who Moved My Cheese?* as one of the six all-time books that every business person should read. We've included key content from that work in this book (and in our online course) for you.

As you can tell from the name *Strategic Acceleration,* strategy is obviously the key to optimizing the Clarity, Focus, and Execution formula introduced in that book. The word *strategy* is quite misused, and I've found that many people don't understand it. Most think of it as a business word, and yet they go through life not being *Intentionally Strategic* in either their business or their personal lives. I believe you can be *Intentionally Strategic* about your health (as you can see in my book *Ultimate Health*); you can be *Intentionally Strategic* about raising your kids (see my book *Strategic Parenting* on this subject); and you can be *Intentionally Strategic* about getting advice (see my book *Advice Matters*).

Let me take just a moment and share with you an example of how I've been strategic in both parenting and seeking advice. I've been fortunate to raise two incredible daughters. Much of the credit, obviously, goes to my wife and to our parents. However, I was also very strategic about reaching out to three other couples who had daughters around ten years older than ours and having them strategically pour into our thinking the things they did successfully in parenting and the improvements they would have made in raising their daughters. As parents, we were able to take advantage of their advice and pull distinctions that made a positive impact on our kids. People often think of mentors in a business framework, and they often don't think about having a mentor to help them be strategic in raising their kids or getting better results in all areas of their lives. Having one or more mentors is just one area where you can be strategic, and it can make a huge impact on your success.

**We've put together this book to dramatically impact your success. The content has been organized in a way that will help you digest it one bite at a time.** The heart of the book is the three-step "magic formula" we developed and have proven out over and over through the years: Clarity, Focus, and Execution. We bookended the formula on the front end with the first chapter, "Strategic Mindset," which gives you the foundation for creating extraordinary results by changing how you think, examining what you believe, and adjusting your *Strategic IQ*. Then a chapter is devoted to each of the three steps of the formula—Clarity, Focus, and Execution—with powerful sub-pieces that form the root of the magic formula. Then the far side of the bookend is threefold. First is a chapter on "force multipliers" that shows you how to maximize your efforts as you put the formula to work with above-and-beyond preparation and relationships and by leveraging great tools. Then we include a chapter on utilizing brand, persuasion, and team building to become what everyone wants to be in a variety of ways in their life—a great leader, whether it's for their kids, for their team members, or for an entire company. Then the last chapter teaches how to live a life of Mastery, both personally and professionally, by having great standards and habits and by putting together a team of people to help you in life.

When you get to the chapter on Leadership, you'll see that I teach leaders to create visual models that help others remember their brand and their message. You've probably noticed that we've created one— the Bullseye—that we use throughout the book. The Bullseye is a crisp representation of twenty-one of my most powerful lessons, divided into seven clear areas, with focus on the three-step formula for getting the exact results you want and getting them fast by pulling all the right pieces together. That's what we do—and that's why we've entitled the book *RESULTS Faster!* You'll see this Bullseye come to life in each of the seven chapters and the three lessons within each chapter. They are the right pieces that will guide your arrow to the right results. By the time you complete the book and/or the course you will have my best thinking from my entire life's study on how to get the right results faster.

That's what I do—I'm an encourager, and I'm all about making others better! When you're ready to be extraordinary, both personally and professionally, read this book through to the very last page. I believe it will change your life. If you're not ready for improvement, then please don't turn a single page, and put the book down until another time. You see, when you do read it for the first time, I want it to hit the Bullseye. I want it to strike a chord right in the middle of your being that creates a desire to have nothing less than the best results for your life.

Reading is a great way to absorb new information, and that's why I've authored so many books, including this one. We've found that many people, once they read my books, want to come to my private studio in DFW and spend one-on-one time with me and my hand-picked team. However, time just doesn't allow the capacity to do that for everyone, so we've come up with a medium that fits between reading the book and being in my studio, and that is the online course we've developed. We've teamed up with SUCCESS Partners, which includes *SUCCESS* Magazine and SUCCESS Academy, to publish this book and put together the life-changing course.

For over a decade now I've had a great, special relationship with Stewart Johnson, the owner of SUCCESS Partners. I've been coaching him and his team, and I'm very happy to be part of the SUCCESS family as he continues to grow his enterprises. As a result of my relationship with Stewart and the SUCCESS entities, my works have blossomed into a staple in their Academy. I've been a columnist for

*SUCCESS* Magazine for years, so I want to also encourage you to read the magazine, whether electronically or through hard copy, and I invite you to get connected to my column, "Ask The RESULTS Guy™."

We've now combined our efforts in these two works so we can deeply impact others, including you as the reader. We've invested over $100,000 developing a course that expands on the content of this book, which is the next best thing to being right in my studio. For now, I hope you enjoy the content of the book and that it makes a powerful impact on your results.

If you like what you read, certainly sign up and go through the course (see details at the end of the book on how to sign up) and/or come and say "Hi" to me in person and invest time with me in the *Strategic Acceleration Studio* (contact my team at info@tonyjeary. com). Either way, "Cheers to *RESULTS Faster!*" Now, let's get underway.

## CHAPTER 1:

# STRATEGIC MINDSET

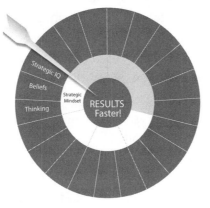

This book is about being successful, making money, and being happy—succeeding in all the areas of your life that matter most to you, both personally and professionally.

Everyone has a next level. Everyone has their own par. Everyone can compress their vision to reality faster with the right formula, and I am going to give that to you—right here and right now. The very best top achievers, those who have extraordinary results in their life, are *Intentionally Strategic* in all areas of their life. I'm going to show you how to do that!

> THE VERY BEST TOP ACHIEVERS, THOSE WHO HAVE EXTRAORDINARY RESULTS IN THEIR LIFE, ARE *INTENTIONALLY STRATEGIC* IN ALL AREAS OF THEIR LIFE.

You may be starting from scratch and feeling overwhelmed with your day-to-day responsibilities. Maybe you're in transition, or you're going through a big change in your life or your career. Perhaps you're currently achieving at a high level, and you'd like to enjoy life at an even higher level. Or maybe you simply need or want proven strategies and tools to deal with the pace of change in today's world. Wherever you are in your life or career, you'll find what you need in this book to go to the next level.

Sixteen years ago I had a multi-million-dollar international consulting firm with offices in China, L.A., Detroit, and Dallas, and I was making millions of dollars and impacting people's lives. When I would fly home on the weekends, though, I would sit down in my living room and see my kids for a few hours before they would go to sleep; and during those few hours I was thinking, "I'm here with them, and yet I'm actually not because I'm out of energy." Can you relate to that? Is your calendar so full that you're not creating the results you want? I said to myself, *From a results perspective, I want to have extraordinary kids. I want to have an incredible life. That means I have to be careful about putting too much energy in bouncing all around the world and not pouring it into my kids.* So I stepped back and said, *I need to change my model, and I need to change some things about my life so I can live the life that I want to live.* And I did just that.

Today I work out of my back yard on my estate. People fly in from all over the world so I can advise them, change their thinking, and advance their goals to reality quicker. That's very powerful! And many other good things have happened on top of that! I've been happily married for twenty-five years; I have two beautiful, extraordinary kids; and I now have a son-in-law who is as happy and giving and cheerful as my two daughters. I have the privilege of working with some of the top achievers in the world. As a matter of fact, I've worked with over 1,000 clients. Presidents of companies like Sam's, American Airlines, HP, Firestone, Samsung, and New York Life come right here to my studio.

As a matter of fact, even the president of Walmart, who flew here in his jet, has sat right here in my studio to let me help him strategize and plan his future. I've authored over forty books, developed hundreds of courses in multiple languages, and worked on six continents and in forty-five countries. I live a blessed life!

And yet it hasn't always been that way. I've been broke, I've been embezzled, I've been sued, and I've been overweight. I was so broke at one time that I had to hire a former bankruptcy attorney to protect me from being forced into involuntary bankruptcy. Now that's living on the edge, isn't it?

I tell you this because I want you to know right up front that I live everything I am about to give to you to the extreme. I've seen many authorities in my life—and maybe you have, too—who write books, speak, and train, and yet they themselves were not doing what they suggested. I have studied the world of success more than most anybody I know, and I want to share my learnings with you through my partnership with SUCCESS Academy.

Throughout this book, in almost every chapter, we're going to be talking about thinking. Since the mind is the engine of action, we ultimately become and do what we think. So if the results you're getting are less than you want or expect, you need to develop a new way of thinking about what it takes to be successful, in both your professional and personal life. To get better results, you have to have better execution; and better execution comes from knowing the right actions to take. And the best way to know what actions to take is to have the right mindset—a *Strategic Mindset*.

As you read this book, I am going to push you to think and reflect, and I am going to encourage you throughout the entire journey. You see, I enjoy helping people thrive. I enjoy impacting people's lives, and that means you!

Over the years I've refined this methodology to a high level. In 2006, we conducted personal interviews with over thirty of our best, long-term customers to help me understand what I was precisely doing to help them achieve greater success. I used this information to help me hone in on, further define, and sharpen the strategies, tools, and resources I'm going to share with you in this book—highly effective, proven strategies and a system to help you get results.

The basis for the methodology I am sharing with you is founded upon what I call *Strategic Acceleration*—a system that will show you how to think differently, because changing your thinking is going to change your results.

## THREE-STEP FORMULA

This system of thinking is based on a very simple yet powerful three-step formula that forms the foundation for this program. The three elements of *Strategic Acceleration* are Clarity, Focus, and Execution.

**Clarity**: Understanding your vision and knowing exactly what you want. There's a pulling power that comes from clarity, and we want to bring that to life.

**Focus**: I know and coach so many people all over the world (and this could be you) who burn up five, ten, and twenty hours a week in distractions. I want to show you how to be focused so you're concentrating on what matters and filtering out what doesn't.

**Execution**: We all have to take action to get accelerated results with powerful accountability.

## TWO BASIC NEEDS

Both individuals and organizations have two basic needs in order to be successful at the very highest level—the need for speed and the need for results! Things are changing so rapidly in today's world that we need to have a way to not only cope with these changes, but to also use them to our advantage. And the primary principle of success today is speed!

The speed of life changes things. Think about it. Everyone is on Facebook. LinkedIn is the new Rolodex. YouTube is the new T.V. If you ask a kid to look up something in an encyclopedia, they look on Google to see what an encyclopedia is. Right? That's the world we live in today.

We live in a fast-paced world. We must think differently to accomplish greater results. There are opportunities everywhere, and yet there is also plenty of pressure—about how to spend your time and where to put your resources.

We have a proven formula that will help you become a better person, a better leader, a better team member, a better contributor and, in fact, a better results achiever.

## Two Biggest Takeaways

This is the bottom line of where we're headed in this book. I'm giving you the two biggest takeaways, right up front:

1. *High Leverage Activities* (HLAs). No single skill or habit has a more powerful impact on results than the ability to eliminate distractions and focus on your High Leverage Activities. You absolutely have to take this one away.

2. You must be *Intentionally Strategic* about everything you do, including your HLAs.

If you want to play at the Mastery level, you have to get these two right.

Studies show that small actions taken consistently are much more effective than eating the whole whale in one bite. I encourage you to come back to this book from time to time and review it over and over, because you pick up new distinctions and nuances each time you do. And for even better results, you might consider signing up for the RESULTS Faster! online course or contacting me about coming to my studio to learn firsthand how to move to the next level in your results.

## Results Audit

Peter Drucker is one of my all-time guys I admire. He did so many cool things with MBO—management by objectives—and one of the things he said and is known for was, "What gets measured gets improved." So let's do an exercise right now to measure where you are currently, and then at the end of the book we'll measure again to see how much you've improved by absorbing the concepts I've introduced in this book.

Look at the RESULTS Faster! Audit on the next three pages. I'd like for you to go through all seven areas—Strategic Mindset, Clarity, Focus, Execution, Force Multipliers, Leadership, and Mastery—and rate yourself between one and five on each one to see where you currently are. A one means you're not where you want to be, and a five means you have already mastered that area.

Chances are, if you're like most people, you're probably a two or three in most of the areas. And that's phenomenal, because now you know exactly where you are, and you can work on your progress. If you were lower or higher in a couple of areas, that's fine, too. What we want to do is push those numbers up by the time you finish reading and studying the principles and ideas in this book.

# THE RESULTS AUDIT: BEFORE

*What gets measured, gets improved.*
—PETER DRUCKER

Please take a few moments and rate yourself on this simple self-audit of where you currently operate in each of the seven primary areas covered in this book. 1 is low, 5 is high. Check the level you think best represents your current level of mastery in each area. If your results are lower than you'd like, don't worry! This is exactly what we'll be exploring in this course. Knowing precisely where you are now gives you a clear map for where you want to be.

| Module 1 | Level 1 | Level 2 | Level 3 | Level 4 | Level 5 |
|---|---|---|---|---|---|
| **Strategic Thinking:** *How intentional am I at managing my thinking?*<br><br>**My Rating:** | I don't know how to manage my thinking or what my beliefs are. I focus mostly on activities, and I'm very busy all the time. | I realize that my thoughts can affect my productivity, and beliefs influence my actions. I'd like to be more strategic in what I do. | I practice thinking strategically, and I have identified many of my good and bad beliefs. I assess my day based on what I believe will produce the best results. | My thoughts are mostly directive and purposeful. I actively work to eliminate false beliefs while strengthening beliefs that keep me focused. My days are focused and productive. | I use my thoughts strategically to guide me toward my goals. I live an authentic life based on my chosen beliefs. I consistently ask, "What's the best use of my time right now?" |

| Module 2 | Level 1 | Level 2 | Level 3 | Level 4 | Level 5 |
|---|---|---|---|---|---|
| **Clarity:** *How clear am I about what's important in my life and work?* <br><br> **My Rating:** | I have very little idea about my life's purpose, passions, what makes me happy, or my values or goals. | I believe in having a clear picture of what's important in life, including my passion, purpose, and what makes me happy. I think about my values and have one or two clear goals. | I know what's important to me in life, including my values and goals. I'm putting some of my values into practice, and I am implementing written action plans for my goals. | I am motivated by my list of purpose, passion, values, and goals, and I am following a clear plan to create a life designed around what's most important to me. | My purpose, passion, values, and goals guide my daily decisions and actions. I am absolutely clear on the results I will achieve and how I choose to live. |

| Module 3 | Level 1 | Level 2 | Level 3 | Level 4 | Level 5 |
|---|---|---|---|---|---|
| **Focus:** *How focused am I in my life and work?* <br><br> **My Rating:** | I find myself easily distracted and/or bogged down in insignificant, time-consuming tasks. I say "yes" too often to other people's priorities. | I am working to improve my focusing skills. I know what I need to do more of and less of to be more productive, and I'm figuring out my High-Leverage Activities (HLAs). I try to say "yes" only to what matters most. | I prioritize the things I need to do more of and delegate what I can. I focus on activities that will produce the greatest results and usually have the courage to say "no" to other priorities. | Each day I focus on things that are relevant to my strategic agenda, success, and achievement. I accomplish my daily HLAs 80% of the time and say "no" to anything that does not match these activities. | I concentrate solely on completing strategic goals and objectives. I am more productive than ever and deliver outstanding results on time or early. |

| Module 4 | Level 1 | Level 2 | Level 3 | Level 4 | Level 5 |
|---|---|---|---|---|---|
| **Execution:** *How well do I manage my time and effort to get things done?*<br><br>**My Rating:** | I procrastinate and have trouble delivering results on time and fail to ask others for help because I am not a good communicator. | I am somewhat better at getting things done on time. I occasionally call in more resources to help, but I need to get better at enrolling others. | I schedule my time effectively, and ask for help/additional resources early. I am comfortable in sharing my ideas and viewpoints with others and understanding their needs. | I execute my plans and deliver results on time. I am good at recruiting and encouraging others, giving value, and helping them get what they want as they help me get what I want. | I am exceptional in exceeding expectations and delivering results on time or early. I communicate brilliantly with others, and I move them to take action so we all produce results faster. |

| Module 5 | Level 1 | Level 2 | Level 3 | Level 4 | Level 5 |
|---|---|---|---|---|---|
| **Force Multipliers:** *How well do I use leverage to get things done faster and more efficiently?*<br><br>**My Rating:** | I tend to do everything myself, and I have trouble getting things done. My preparation is poor. | I use some tools to help me out, and I'm getting better at preparing and reaching out to others for help. I spend time in advance to get ready for big projects or events. | I often use tools, preparation, and my network to help me achieve results faster. | I seek out and use the best tools, people, and strategies to help leverage my own efforts. I prepare relentlessly for any opportunity I'm presented with. | I leverage my efforts in multiple ways and through my extensive network of connections. Preparation is part of my daily practice, and my results are spectacular. |

| Module 6 | Level 1 | Level 2 | Level 3 | Level 4 | Level 5 |
|---|---|---|---|---|---|
| **Leadership:** *How well do I nourish and foster the environments that support extraordinary decision making?* <br><br> **My Rating:** | I may have a vision, but I don't communicate it well. People have little confidence in my leadership because they don't really know who I am. | I have articulated a vision to my team, and they understand what we want to achieve. I am clear about my strengths, and I want to help my team develop theirs. | The team is inspired by the goals and vision I communicate to them. I discover what my team wants and then encourage their efforts to succeed. | The team is self-directed and focused, and my job as leader is simply to empower them to excel. We are achieving great things together. | The team has produced outstanding results, and they attribute much of our success to my support and leadership. |

| Module 7 | Level 1 | Level 2 | Level 3 | Level 4 | Level 5 |
|---|---|---|---|---|---|
| **Mastery:** *How committed am I to consistently produce extraordinary results?* <br><br> **My Rating:** | I know I need better standards and habits, and I could use much more support from others. | I am learning how to get better results in life and business. I've created powerful standards, and I'm building habits to make those standards real. I've started to locate a team to help me out. | Every day I measure myself against my standards and work to ingrain good habits even deeper into my life. I have a group of experts to call upon when I need them. | I focus on raising my standards, exceeding my own expectations, and reinforcing my good habits daily. I leverage as much as I can to others who do an exceptional job in their fields, so I can do the same in mine. | I consistently produce extraordinary results in my life and business—that is the standard I live by. My good habits drive my results and success, and my *Life Team* makes what I do possible. |

By taking this audit at the beginning of the book and then again at the end, I think you'll see that you've already moved the needle significantly toward RESULTS Faster!

In the rest of this chapter, we're going to cover the three most important aspects of *Strategic Mindset* that can powerfully affect your results: your thinking, your beliefs, and what I call your *Strategic IQ.*

# THINKING

The foundation of the entire *RESULTS Faster!* book and online course is right here! You may remember my telling you in the Introduction about Jim Norman, a man who will always be very special to me. Let me tell you how he impacted my life.

In 1991, Chrysler was going on its last hope. Lee Iacocca was leaving, and they needed to turn the company around. I invested the next five years of my life helping put Chrysler on the front cover of *Forbes* Magazine as one of the most admired companies in America. It changed my career.

About twenty years or so ago, I was flying to Detroit to work with Chrysler. I looked over and saw Zig Ziglar, and Jim Norman was sitting next to him. I knelt down in the aisle to talk to both of them. For about twenty minutes, we had quite an interesting conversation. I discovered that Zig and Jim were also going to Chrysler, so I explained Chrysler's entire organizational chart to them. They were impressed. Needless to say, that was the start of an exceptional experience.

A few weeks later I got a call from Jim, asking me how I could help Zig get more into the corporate world. They ended up hiring me, and that relationship went on for many years. A year and a half later, Jim left his position as president of Zig's organization and started his own consulting company. I was his first client out of the chute, as he became my coach, and we ended up having a twenty-year relationship. During the first ten years I continuously and persistently asked him to be my president, because he was an incredible thinker. It was obvious in what he had done for Zig and what he had done in his past life as an entrepreneur.

In 2006, after ten years of my begging him, he agreed to come in as my president. That's when he told me, "Tony, one of the things that you do so well is you help people think; and you know, thinking is not easy." I said "Jim, I don't think you're right. Thinking is not that hard. Everyone does it." He said, "No, thinking is not easy." I thought a long time about what he had said, and I finally realized that he was right. Thinking is not easy.

Think about your own life. Are you constantly doing, or do you step back and think enough? Most people don't think, and I want to tell you right up front that there's a ton of power toward getting results faster by thinking more impactfully.

EVERY PROBLEM IS A THINKING PROBLEM.

**High achievers want results. They want to win, and they're often faced with problems. One of those problems is that they want results faster.** That may be what you're facing, as well. You see, every problem is a thinking problem. So what do you do when you don't get the results you want, or when you don't get the results you want fast enough? I suggest you make some changes.

Let me share with you another story. The president of a public company hired me a year and a half ago and said, "One of the things I want you to do is help my executives think more." He said, "I want one of their *High Leverage Activities* to be thinking so we can go to another level." After that year and a half, the company's market capitalization went up over 30 percent—by $500 million dollars!

Thinking is so powerful, and most people don't do enough of it.

## INTENTIONAL THINKING

This is not the barely conscious thinking we do most of the time, like when we're shopping for groceries or driving the same way to work every day. That kind of thinking is second nature. I'm talking about the intentional thinking it takes to solve problems. As I said, every problem is a thinking problem. We use intentional thinking to look at all the pieces and make strategic decisions. That means we have to let go of old thought patterns and be open to new ways of thinking.

Our world changes daily, and it doesn't take long for knowledge to become outdated, for skills to weaken, or for paradigms to shift. Unless we're willing, as Abraham Lincoln once said, to "think anew and act anew," we're likely to make very poor choices. We have to constantly check our thinking to make sure it hasn't become outdated.

How you think affects what you can or can't accomplish. Wealthy people think differently from those who have little wealth. Successful people usually focus on how something can be done, while unsuccessful people think about why it can't be done.

---

Intentional thinkers adopt three kinds of thinking:

1. No excuses thinking. You're not after excuses; you're after results.

2. Solution-oriented thinking. Ask "How do we?" instead of saying, "Here's why we can't."

3. Long-term thinking. Look beyond the immediate future or even the future beyond that, and consider what you want to accomplish five, ten, or even twenty years from now.

---

And there's one kind of thinking that intentional thinkers avoid at all costs—negative thinking. Negative thoughts clutter our minds and use the same mental real estate that positive ones do. You wouldn't keep garbage in your living space, so why would you keep a negative thought in your brain?

How well do you think? Do you think often enough? Are you intentional enough? Do you have inputs into your thinking? Reflect on the types of thinking I just mentioned, and ask yourself these questions:

1. Where in your life do you need to apply no-excuses thinking?

2. Where in your life do you need to apply solution-oriented thinking?

3. Where in your life do you need to apply long-term thinking? What will happen when you do?

4. Where in your life do you need to eliminate negative thinking? How much better will you feel if you recognize negative thoughts and sweep them out like garbage?

Intentional thinking is a big deal! Let me suggest eight ways to help you think more intentionally.

## Eight Ways to Improve Your Thinking

1. **Determine your talents.** Work in your sweet spot. Do you know what your strengths are and the strengths of your team, and are you all living in them daily?

2. **Surround yourself with the right people.** If you want to think better, then intentionally surround yourself with smart thinkers. Who you spend time with is who you become.

3. **Timing**. Sometimes the timing might not be right, and you need to say "No." Knowing when to take action and when not to is so important. And sometimes you may need to say to yourself, *You know, I need to stop before I make a decision and let my intuition kick into gear. I need to think about the situation before I take action or before I make a decision.*

> **IF YOU WANT TO THINK BETTER, THEN INTENTIONALLY SURROUND YOURSELF WITH SMART THINKERS.**

4. **Daily discipline**. I ask myself this question all the time: *What is the best use of my time right now?* I think about it eight, ten, or twelve times a day, and you should too. Having the discipline to say, *What's the best use of my time?* is a very powerful thinking tool that I would encourage you to put into your habits.

5. **Attention to detail**. I was fortunate to grow up in my family business, which was cleaning and detailing cars. Why is that important? I grew up with my parents and grandparents teaching me how to look at every detail, so I developed the habit of looking at every detail when I go into anything. For example, if I'm going to a meeting, I make sure I have my notes down so I'm thinking smart before I get there.

6. **Risk tolerance.** So many people are not clear on their risk tolerance, whether it involves investing or activities. For example, when you're flying down the mountain on skis, you might look over and see people skiing next to trees and going over moguls. They're living in danger land. Well, that's not where I want to be. My risk tolerance is not that high. Yes, I like adventure; however, I don't want to be messed up. I think all the time about my risk tolerance in everything I do, and I would encourage you to do the same thing. Know your risk tolerance in all areas of your life.

> ASK YOURSELF EIGHT, TEN, OR TWELVE TIMES A DAY, *WHAT IS THE BEST USE OF MY TIME RIGHT NOW?*

7. **Energy is everything!** Think about how you maintain and manage your energy. For example, what you eat, your environment, and even the music you listen to can have a huge impact on your thinking. I have things in my office environment that spike my energy and push me up—like pictures of my kids that fire me up—so I can be energetic, whether I am making decisions, negotiating, or impacting someone.

8. **Long-terming**. When my son-in-law asked me if he could marry my daughter, I said "yes," and then I immediately said, "We need to start praying for your grandkids." He was shocked and said, "What?" I said, "We're a generational family, and we need to be thinking long-term about your grandkids." When you're refining your thinking, remember that long-terming can be very powerful.

The bottom line is, thinking is a strategic asset. When you recognize that and manage your thinking accordingly, incredible things become possible. Don't just be a doer; be a strategic thinker and make thinking a big part of your life.

Now let's talk about how your beliefs affect your *Strategic Mindset.*

# BELIEFS

## THE *BELIEF WINDOW*

Whether we realize it or not, we all conduct our lives and make decisions based upon our beliefs. Let me give you an example from my own life.

About five or six years ago I was having breakfast with one of my clients. When I walked in, I could see that he had lost quite a bit of weight, and I said to him, "Ron, you look terrific!" After we talked a while, he said, "You know, once you turn fifty, it's all about what you eat." He said, "You just slammed down three glasses of orange juice. Do you know what the GI is on the orange juice you just drank?" And I said, "What's GI?" I had no idea at that time what glycemic index was. He said, "Do you know what the calorie content of orange juice is?" and I said, "No, I thought orange juice was good for you." He said, "You just drank three glasses of orange juice at 250 calories a pop. That's 750 calories, before you even started to eat your breakfast." I was shocked! I had a belief that orange juice was good for you! I said, "Oh man! I need to look at my health. I need to understand much more than I do." (And I'm going to talk to you more about that later in the book, because I know that's important to all of us. Right?) It is imperative that we have the right beliefs on our window, including the right principles about our health.

**One of the most powerful and impactful models I could ever show you is called the *Belief Window*.** Here's how it works: Principles on your *Belief Window* filter how you see the world. Primarily, we get the principles on our window from our upbringing—our parents. And as we go through life, the experiences, teachers, and relationships we have, as well as the information we get from books, the Internet,

> **WHETHER WE REALIZE IT OR NOT, WE ALL CONDUCT OUR LIVES AND MAKE DECISIONS BASED UPON OUR BELIEFS.**

and other media, keep refining those principles. All of us are doing life right now the very best we can based on our principles.

Sometimes, though, a principle on our window may be wrong. In fact, I believe we're often doing life with principles that are incorrect, just like my belief about the orange juice that I told you about. My belief was that orange juice was healthy for you and that you should drink plenty of it. In the five years since that time, I may have had two glasses of orange juice, because my beliefs now include the right information about GI.

Let me give you another example. Most people, maybe even you, grew up with the idea that you should always clean your plate. Right? Now, think about that. Do you think that's a good principle today? If you always clean your plate today, you probably don't use portion control and you overeat.

Maybe you've changed your eating habits now and you're doing pretty well. Now let me ask you this: Do you ever feel guilty when you don't clean your plate? Many people do, because they still have that principle on their window. We know now, of course, that it's better both to use portion control and to take your plate away once you start getting full. Then your digestive system kicks in, and you feel satisfied. Many people get it when I use this example in talking about the *Belief Window*. Trust me on this one. You could have incorrect principles on your window. If you want the best results in your life, you have to get this one right.

Sometimes we don't correct the principles on our window fast enough to keep up with technology. As technology moves, you have to update the principles on your window. The speed of life is fast. The bottom line here is that you have to make sure you own the beliefs that are on your window.

We all have what are called core beliefs: the things that are truly important to us and that we believe are true about ourselves and the world. Maybe you believe you're a good person or that you work hard. And maybe you believe you're a good parent or child or boss or employee. Think about your core beliefs and take a minute to write them down.

It's important to know our core beliefs, and it's even more important to understand that we can choose new beliefs that will help us be more successful. What are two beliefs you could add that would make it easier for you to get the results you want faster? Here are a few examples: "I'm efficient and effective at whatever I do." "I work well with others and inspire them to be their best." "I love what I do and I'm great at it." Add your two or three new beliefs to the core beliefs you listed before.

> THE MOST SUCCESSFUL PEOPLE IN THE WORLD GOT THAT WAY BECAUSE THEY COPIED THE BELIEFS AND HABITS OF PEOPLE WHO WERE MORE SUCCESSFUL THAN THEY WERE.

Here's a secret for you: The most successful people in the world got that way because they copied the beliefs and habits of people who were more successful than they were!

## BLIND SPOTS, DISTINCTIONS, AND PERSPECTIVES

Now I want to talk to you about *Blind Spots* (those things you don't see), distinctions (looking at the details), and perspectives (the angles from which you're looking).

Let's face it—it's so important that we uncover our *Blind Spots*. Inaccurate principles, missed distinctions, and overlooked perspectives hinder your results.

Let me give you an example that will bring this *Blind Spot* idea to life. Look at the picture of the FedEx truck below.

Now, we see the FedEx logo all of the time, and we've seen it for decades. We see it on their planes. We see it on their trucks. We see it on their packages. We see it on the Internet. Yet when most people look at the FedEx truck, they don't see two things that are right there in front of them. Take a moment and study the logo. Can you see them?

One is a serving spoon and one is an arrow. Most people don't see them unless they've been pointed out to them before.

What this exercise reveals is that we may not even see something that has been right in front of us for a long time. That's what a *Blind Spot* is. It's something you don't see. (That's called a *scotoma* in medical terms.) We want to make sure we do our best to uncover our *Blind Spots* so we can make the most impactful decisions in our life.

And we also want to make sure that the distinctions we have in front of us are the very best. What do you see in the picture below? Do you see a tree, do you see animal heads, or do you see both? We want to make sure we see all of the distinctions that will help us be successful in our business and personal lives.

If there's an area in your life where you're not getting the results you want, it's very likely you have a *Blind Spot* that's getting in your way. Let me give you four very effective ways to identify *Blind Spots:*

1. Actively look for any beliefs that might be sabotaging you.

2. If you're experiencing stress about something, there's probably a belief getting in your way—look to see what the belief is.

3. Check your beliefs to make sure they're up to date. Are you using a year 2000 "operating system" to try and run your 2016 life?

4. Get advice. Ask someone you trust to help you figure out your *Blind Spots.* Let's talk more about that.

## GETTING ADVICE

One of the smartest ways to deal with *Blind Spots,* distinctions, and perspectives is to get advice! If you have the right advice, you can make better decisions, avoid mistakes, plan more effectively, and minimize your risk by uncovering *Blind Spots*—all of which lead to better results.

A friend of mine, Jay Rodgers, recently co-authored a book with me called *Advice Matters*. I met Jay about six years ago, and we hit it off right away. He became my mentor, and then we decided to write a book together. Initially, we wanted to write the book because of our exceptional mentoring relationship; we wanted to help others benefit from the same kind of mentorship. We ended up expanding the book into being more about getting advice than just about mentors. If you have the right advice coming into your beliefs, the principles on your window are going to be more accurate and impactful.

In the book we offer six solutions for dealing with *Blind Spots*, distinctions, and perspectives.

1. Mentors

2. Coaches

3. Trusted colleagues

4. Paid professionals

5. Resources

6. Yourself (self-reflection)

## Mentors

Do you have mentors in your life? A mentor is someone who has done what you want to do or has been where you want to go. Mentors are usually older and more experienced. They're willing to give up their time to offer you free advice and counsel to help you be better. You may remember my story in the Introduction about the incredible mentors I had for fifteen years who poured into our lives and helped my wife and me raise two extraordinary daughters. Mentors will help you have the best principles on your window and will truly affect the way you believe.

## Coaches

I believe in paid coaches. Imagine this: I've had the same coach for thirty years! The CIO of Deloitte was in my studio about five years ago, and I was bragging about my coach, Mark Pantak. At the time, he had been my coach for twenty-five years. My client said, "You're telling me you've had the same guy pouring into your success for twenty-five years of your life, longer than you've been married?" I said "That's right!" That conversation reminded me how fortunate I was, and the next day I went out and bought an iPad and mailed it to Mark with a note that said, "Thank you so much for pouring into my life."

You may have a coach; if you don't, I encourage you to think about getting one. They help you see things you won't normally see. They'll uncover *Blind Spots*. Often a good coach will have an arsenal of tools to share with you. My coach brings me things all the time. He sends me books. He connects me to courses. He gives me insight and helps me bring the best out of myself. Wouldn't you like to have someone in your corner to help you advance your career and get results faster?

## TRUSTED COLLEAGUES

These are people you work with or maybe you've worked with in the past, and at some point in your relationship you've realized that you can trade out ideas. I have six or eight trusted colleagues I exchange ideas with regularly. In fact, I call them my informal board. For example, if I'm doing a new book, I might forward several book cover ideas to them and ask, "Which one of these do you like best?" They send me an e-mail with their insights, and maybe even uncover a *Blind Spot* or two that I might not be seeing in the book cover choices. They send me messages from time to time asking for my input on their work, and I'll send them my insights.

I encourage you to find several trusted colleagues who can be helpful to you in trading insights and advice, who can give you perspective by helping you see details and distinctions, and who can help you go to another level.

## PAID PROFESSIONALS

These are people like attorneys or CPAs who you pay to give you specific advice so you can make better decisions. Because of their knowledge and expertise, they can often uncover *Blind Spots* that you may not see.

## RESOURCES

You can find excellent advice from resources like books, audios, DVDs, URLs, periodicals like *SUCCESS* magazine, and even TED Talks and YouTube. Are you pouring resources like these into your mind so you can get advice from some of the best experts in the world? These are excellent tools to help you make the best decisions and constantly be refining the distinctions and principles on your *Belief Window*. Build your resources!

## YOURSELF

Taking the time to step back and reflect on your past achievements and ways you can improve is so valuable. Giving advice to yourself, reflecting, and thinking through challenges and ideas is something most people don't do enough of.

We all have *Blind Spots,* distinctions, and perspectives we need to deal with, and the best way to ensure we have the right beliefs or principles on our *Belief Window* is to get the right advice from the right places.

Now let me show you how to take your thinking to a whole new level by improving what I call your Strategic IQ.

# STRATEGIC IQ

## THINKING STRATEGICALLY

The most successful people don't dwell on problems; they live in solutions. We all know that change happens fast and often without warning and that problems do exist. Yet change can also create opportunities to provide solutions to problems.

I want to show you how to think strategically at a whole new level that focuses on solutions rather than problems. Often our inclination is to develop a tactical response to a perceived problem, when we need to be strategic.

Let me give you an example. A sales person's tactical approach to change might be to sharpen their cold-calling script. That's pretty tactical. A better strategic approach might be to learn about the prospect's problems and offer tailored solutions. You see, having that balance between thinking and doing is very powerful.

How about on the home front? Suppose you want your family to eat healthier food. A tactical approach might be to take a low-fat cooking class or get a new health food cookbook, or even throw out all the junk food. These are wonderful approaches—but how could you approach it more strategically? Maybe you could come up with a way to get your family to think more about nutrition. Strategic thinking often leads to long-term solutions rather short-term.

## TACTICAL VERSUS STRATEGIC

What's the difference between tactical and strategic? Tactical involves things like tasks, calls, activities, and paperwork. Strategic involves things like planning, thinking, and studying. When my coach and former president Jim Norman said, "Thinking is hard," he was talking about strategic thinking.

Just to stimulate your thinking, write down what percentage of the time you and/or your team operate in the tactical, and what percentage of the time you and/or your team operate in the strategic. Those two numbers should add up to 100 percent.

We've found that most people need to be more strategic. How about you? Was your tactical percentage pretty high? And we have found some who are too strategic. They plan, plan, plan, and then they plan some more. If that's you, you probably don't take enough action. As I go around the world, I find that about 90 percent of the people are so tactical that they're busy doing and doing and not strategically looking at all the pieces of the puzzle. I want to push you to think at that level.

*Strategic IQ* is about balancing that out. An executive doing her own PowerPoints is an example of being too tactical. If I owned stock in a company and I saw an executive doing her own PowerPoints, I would think, *With the kind of money we're paying this executive to run a company, do we want her doing her own PowerPoints? No, we don't!*

*We want her lifting up and being strategic, looking at all the pieces. What can the company acquire? Who can it attract? What can it move?* I would want her thinking and planning at the top level! Right? So many people are too tactical, doing things at the lower level when they should be more strategic.

Ask yourself this question often: *What's the best use of my time right now?* I mentioned that question earlier, and I want to drill it home right now. Sometimes the answer should be tactical, and sometimes it should be strategic. If you have an extra few minutes before or after a meeting, I encourage you to look at your list on your phone to see what you have going on and ask yourself, *Do I need to be doing something tactical, like sending an e-mail or following up on a call? Or do I need to lift up and look at my week or my month and see how things are going? Do I need to renegotiate or allocate more resources on something to make sure everything happens for that day, that week, that month, or that year?* People miss this, and I want you to own it. Constantly ask yourself, *What's the best use of my time right now?*

> **ASK YOURSELF THIS QUESTION OFTEN: WHAT'S THE BEST USE OF MY TIME RIGHT NOW? SOMETIMES THE ANSWER SHOULD BE TACTICAL, AND SOMETIMES IT SHOULD BE STRATEGIC.**

In the next chapter, we explore the first step in my proven three-step *Strategic Acceleration* formula—Clarity. Authentic vision has the power to pull you out of your circumstances and toward a better life and better results. This pulling power comes from having complete clarity about what you truly want. Clarity opens up new opportunities and connections and empowers you to better make strategic choices that will lead to superior results faster.

# V.I.P.s

- Change your thinking, change your results.

- Every problem is a thinking problem, so thinking is a strategic asset.

- Ensure the principles on your *Belief Window* are true, accurate, and current—not outdated, not off mark, and not false!

- The most successful people in the world got that way because they copied the beliefs and habits of people who were more successful than they were.

- Not only balance tactical and strategic, but also be *Intentionally Strategic* about everything if you want the right results faster.

- Ask yourself this question often: *What's the best use of my time right now?* Sometimes the answer should be tactical, and sometimes it should be strategic.

# CHAPTER 2:

# CLARITY

Now we're going to dig into the formula that forms the foundation of this entire program, and it's based upon my best-selling book, *Strategic Acceleration*. Let me set the stage by telling you how it all started.

You may remember my telling you about my friend Jim Norman, who was also my coach and my president. When he started helping me as president of my company in 2006, we did the research to find out what people were getting most from my services. As a result of our findings, we decided to develop a little book called *The Passport to Strategic Acceleration*. I printed 10,000 copies and sent out 5,000 of them to various organizations. Just a few days later I got a call from the Sergeant at Arms of the US Senate in Washington, D.C., who basically said, "Tony, we need clarity, focus, and execution up here in the Senate." So I flew to Washington. Now, though I can't tell you they listened to me, I can tell you they got fired up over the Clarity, Focus, and Execution formula—so much so, in fact, that I flew back home and said to Jim, "I believe we're onto something here." He said "No, this is not something new; this is what you do."

We ended up flying to New York together to talk to one of my agents. We turned the formula into a full-fledged best-selling book, and *Strategic Acceleration* was launched. Now, let me remind you again that this is based upon the distinctions I picked up from working with the presidents of such companies as Firestone, Omni, New York Life, TGI Fridays, Ford, and Walmart. After advising and working beside the top people at those successful companies for many years, I realized that's what I helped them do—get clarity for themselves and their teams, get everyone focused, and then execute well.

In the process of working with these top CEOs I discovered that the three enemies of speed and results are:

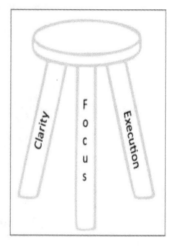

1. Absence of clarity

2. Lack of focus

3. Poor execution

Hence the formula: Clarity, Focus, and Execution—the three legs to the stool, if you will. If one leg is missing, the stool (organization) will collapse.

Clarity is about understanding the vision—where you're going personally and/or professionally. On a scale of one to ten, how clear are you?

How focused are you? Are you tied up with constant distractions, or are you relatively focused?

How about execution? If you want results, you have to execute! Are you taking the action you should?

Clarity, Focus, and Execution!

# CLARITY

The basic definition of clarity is having an unfettered view of your vision of what you want and why you want it, fed by an understanding of its purpose and value. It's about developing a clear vision, outlining priorities and objectives, and tackling goals with a real sense of urgency and focus. Clarity is achieved when ideas and concepts are clearly explained and presented internally and externally, and when you know where you are in relation to where you want to go.

> CLARITY IS ACHIEVED WHEN IDEAS AND CONCEPTS ARE CLEARLY EXPLAINED AND PRESENTED INTERNALLY AND EXTERNALLY, AND WHEN YOU KNOW WHERE YOU ARE IN RELATION TO WHERE YOU WANT TO GO.

Sometimes you may think you have clarity when you actually haven't put much thought into your vision at all. You haven't asked yourself, *What do I truly want and why do I want it?* Not being clear at the outset will have a huge impact as you go about attempting to reach your goals and realize your vision.

Here are four symptoms of poor clarity:

1. You don't believe you can do what you have to do. This is usually because you don't have clarity about what you truly want.

2. You use planning to avoid taking action. Preparation and planning are important, and yet excessive preparation is nothing more than procrastination. Clarity destroys procrastination because the action you need to take is vividly clear.

3. You get stuck or resist leaving your comfort zone. Change isn't always easy; and unless you're willing to change, you will hang onto what's comfortable. Clarity inspires people to be willing to leave the familiar behind for something better.

4. You quit or give up in the face of adversity or difficulty. Clarity of vision gives you the mental substance to persevere and overcome

obstacles. If you're not clear about what you truly want, your belief in your effort will not be powerful or compelling enough to sustain your efforts. When you lack clarity, you will find yourself being pushed toward living in problems.

**GO AS FAR AS YOU CAN SEE IN THIS FAST-PACED WORLD, AND THEN YOU CAN SEE FARTHER.**

Without a clear vision, you're just travelling and rarely arriving. A clear vision pulls and energizes you toward getting what you want. I suggest you go as far as you can see in this fast-paced world, and then you can see farther. When you get more clarity as the weeks and months go, you can make any tweaks or changes that are needed.

Each year Inc. magazine publishes a list of the 5,000 fastest growing companies in the United States. The list is filled with companies of all sizes working across all industries. One of the most important attributes they have in common is a clear vision of what they want to be and accomplish. Getting superior results begins with clarity of vision. When people in a business or organization are clear, the effects are always positive. People know what to do, and they are motivated to action. Clarity becomes the fuel of voluntary change and organizational drive.

There are three pieces to the Clarity puzzle: wealth, values, and goal setting. So let's dive into those elements now and get you on your road to clarity, which will lead you to *Strategic Acceleration*.

# WEALTH

Wealth is way more than just making money to thrive. Wealth is clarity of purpose. It's understanding what makes you happy and what you're passionate about. Wealth is living a happy and healthy lifestyle.

Do you remember the story of Ebenezer Scrooge? He was the miser in Charles Dickens's book *A Christmas Carol* who was very rich—and yet he wasn't wealthy. How about Howard Hughes? When Hughes died in 1976 he was one of the richest men in the world; yet, he was malnourished, filthy, and had no friends or family. He had shut himself off from the world for decades. Howard Hughes was rich—and yet he wasn't wealthy.

What is wealth to you? Do you have clarity? What are you passionate about? What gets you excited? Wealth is about developing a life where every day is a weekend. That's the life I live, and that's the life I want you to live. Wealth is about living on purpose, doing things that make you happy, and living your passion.

A friend of mine, Marty Seligman, wrote a book a few years ago called *Flourish*. It's a very powerful book and one I recommend. Marty has studied happiness for years, and in his book he talks about the five things that everyone wants in order to flourish:

1. Great relationships
2. Accomplishments
3. Engagement
4. Positive emotion
5. Meaning.

I, too, have thought about and done research for years about what we all want, and I've refined my findings into what I believe are the nine elements everyone wants—I took Marty's five and built them into nine. If you truly want to live in flow, you want to live in these nine elements. I've put them into a mnemonic called S.T.R.A.T.E.G.I.C.

**S**ignificance*

**T**ime

**R**elationships*

**A**ccomplishments*

**T**hriving

**E**ngagement*

**G**ood health

**I**nspired*

**C**apital

(Marty's original five are marked with asterisks.)

Think about what you want as we go over each one of the nine elements of happiness.

1. **S** ignificance: Everyone wants to have meaning. I encourage you to think about what it would look like for you to have a level of impact and meaning that would give you real happiness. When I had breakfast with one of my mentors a few years ago, he told me about a discussion he had had with his CPA. His CPA told him that often when people he represented sold their companies, their level of happiness went down within a matter of two years, because they lost the meaning and significance they had when they were driving their business. Significance is important.

2. **T** ime: I find that many people are going around and around on a hamster wheel, and they don't have the *margin time* to travel where they want to go or spend time with the people they want to be with. They don't have flexibility because their calendars are so full. I believe that part of wealth is having that *margin time*. Think about it. Poor time management—not being clear on your *High Leverage Activities*—will put you in a position where you're not living the life you want to live. You have to manage time.

3. **R** elationships: If you have rich relationships, you're going to have an extraordinary life. Think about your relationship with God, your spouse, your kids, your family, your friends, your business associates, your partners, your customers, and your audience or clients. Identifying the roles you play in your life and nourishing those relationships can have a big impact on your happiness.

> **IF YOU HAVE RICH RELATIONSHIPS, YOU'RE GOING TO HAVE AN EXTRAORDINARY LIFE.**

4. **A** ccomplishments: Obviously, everyone wants to accomplish things. Goal achievement actually does create an experience that

leads to happiness. We'll go further in depth about this when we get to goal setting; for now, though, let me give you something to think about: It's not just about what you want to have; it's also about what you want to experience, share, give, and, of course, become.

5. **T hriving**: Every day we want to thrive. We want to flourish. We want to have energy and enjoyment. Do you get up every day, ready to be inspired and thrive in that day? That's something you need to think about when you're defining what happiness means to you.

6. **E ngagement**: Stay engaged! Marty said in his book that the key to having more engagement is to identify your strengths and develop a plan for implementing them in your life. I agree. Do you know what you're good at, and are you travelling in your lane and making sure you're doing those things? If there's something you're not good at, don't do it! Either delegate it to someone else or hire someone to do it so you can spend time doing the things that make you happy.

7. **G ood Health**: Everyone wants good health. As a matter of fact, everyone wants ultimate health. Right? Think about some of the things in your life you need to manage better, like stress and getting enough rest. You want to make sure you have excellent vitals, good tone, and great skin—in fact, all the essentials of ultimate health.

8. **I nspired**: Wouldn't you like to be inspired by your environment and the people around you and have the right state of mind to keep you emotionally high?

9. **C apital**: Financial security is a big deal to most people, and it probably is to you, as well. And of course this includes cash flow. If you have a

> IT'S NOT JUST ABOUT WHAT YOU CAN DO FOR YOURSELF; IT'S ALSO WHAT YOU CAN DO FOR OTHERS.

giant net worth and yet don't have good cash flow, what happens? You get stressed! You have to have cash flow and reserves. And if you want to be truly happy, I encourage you to be a philanthropist and give things away. It's not just about what you can do for yourself; it's also what you can do for others.

## Purpose, Happiness, and Passion

Let's talk about purpose for a minute. In terms of wealth, if you're living on purpose, you're living in the zone. Let me share with you my purpose statement:

> The purpose of my life is to live each day happy and with the Lord, turning people toward God through my words and works, always being a great father, husband, and friend, while giving, improving, and serving all people.

As I'm making decisions every day, I want to live on purpose doing exactly what my purpose statement says. Why do you do what you do? It's very important to get very clear on your purpose.

Now let's look at happiness. When I bring people into my private studio, I encourage them to take the time to write down what makes them the happiest. In fact, why don't you do that right now?

These are the things that make me the happiest: God, wisdom, planning, simplicity, freedom, altruism, health, and travel. I love studying history, being organized and well dressed, and being outdoors in the sunshine. Sometimes I just go outside and soak up the sun. I love my kids and my wife. I love being in serene settings. I love connections, helping people win, being with fun clients, and working with interesting people.

So how about you? Are you absolutely clear on what makes you happy? I encourage you to think about that and write it down.

Finally, if you want to be extremely wealthy, you have to live in your passions. One of the things I am constantly refining with my own coach is what I am passionate about, because I think it changes over time. In order to live a wealthy life, you need to be clear about what your passions are and live them.

Here are my six:

1. Seeing my kids win. Last week when I was out of the country I got a note from my daughter about connecting with a new client. My dream of seeing her understand what I taught her about connections was literally coming true. I had taught her about adding people to her portfolio and winning them with her services. She's a marketing and graphic artist, and seeing her win just put a smile on my face. I know if you have kids, that's important to you as well.

2. Seeing my wife happy. Every year I ask my wife to give me ten things I can do to be a better husband. And you know what she tells me? "Just do the ten I told you to do last year." Seriously, sometimes you need to ask your spouse what makes him or her happy, and that can change over time. I am passionate about making my wife happy.

3. Being with my friends. One of my favorite things to do is to have social activities where I can connect with people that influence my life in a positive way, so I spend time traveling and enjoying dinners and experiences with them.

4. Teaching and advising people. I love helping people win, and that includes you. By doing what I'm doing right now, putting this book together to impact you, I'm doing what I love, and I hope it does deeply impact your life. In fact, I'm hoping you send me a note one day and say "Tony, this book and video course changed my life. It truly did deliver better results for me."

5. Experiencing adventure. I love traveling and seeing the world.

6. Living healthy. I'm passionate about living healthy. As a matter of fact, I work out every day, I eat healthy, and I constantly study to learn how to be better and better.

I encourage you to define wealth for yourself. What does it look like for you to live on purpose, do what makes you happy, and live your passions?

Remember, you are the architect. You can design the life you want. You and you alone have the ability and the power to do that. When you come to a crossroads in your life, you have to define with clarity what you want to have. Will you make it a wealthy life? It's your choice.

> YOU ARE THE ARCHITECT. YOU CAN DESIGN THE LIFE YOU WANT. WHEN YOU COME TO A CROSSROADS IN YOUR LIFE, YOU HAVE TO DEFINE WITH CLARITY WHAT YOU WANT TO HAVE.

# VALUES

A big part of clarity is having clearly defined values so you can make sure your values align with your goals. There's a line from an old poem, "Sea Fever" by John Masefield, that goes, "All I ask is a tall ship/ and a star to steer her by…" Values are the stars that can help steer us to the results we truly want in our lives. What we all actually want is not just results faster—we all want the *right* results faster. That's what we're going to cover in this section.

**A giant mistake that many people make is jumping right into setting their goals and skipping over clarifying their values.** Now everyone needs to be clear on their action plan; there's no doubt about that. And yet most people don't take the time to step back and say, *What is my life all about?*

Your action plan should include your values-based strategy if you want it to endure for the long haul. It's critical to establish clarity about what matters to you, what matters to your spouse if you happen to be married, and what matters for your team if you have a team. You don't want to create results faster and then find out they're the wrong results!

In this section I'm going to help you gain clarity about what your values are so you can match your actions to your values. With clarity, you'll be able to identify areas where you may need to change, and you'll be able to make future decisions simple and clear. When you're able to make a plan that aligns with your values and allows you to focus, your goals will become reality faster.

Let me share a story with you. Remember I'd mentioned earlier that I had a beautiful setup of offices all over the world, and I was making powerful things happen and influencing a ton of people? Well, during that time I was listening to an audio book by Billy Graham, and I heard something from this book that made a massive impact on me. In fact, it changed my life. In the book he poured out his heart to the readers, and one of the things he said was that he had put all of his energy into his ministry and failed at raising his kids. He couldn't take back that time and energy; he missed his opportunity to pour his energy into his kids. I thought, *Here's a guy I greatly admire who truly missed out by not living a powerful piece to his values.* What do you think that said to me? It said that I needed to quit flying all over the world. I needed to be at home and be powerful for my kids. The results I wanted included much more than just money; I wanted my daughters to grow into incredible young adult women. And because I made the changes I needed to make, that's what I have today. My kids have very successfully launched out of the nest. I'm sure you want the same thing if you have kids.

Again, remember that this *RESULTS Faster!* book is not just about making money. It's about getting the results you want in all areas of your life, both personally and professionally.

## What Are Your Values?

Now, what role do your core values play in terms of your setting goals successfully? The first thing you want to do is to have a firm handle on what those values are.

Let me help you do that right up front. Think about this: *What do you enjoy spending time doing? What type of people do you love being around? What makes you feel passionate in life? What moves you emotionally?*

In my case, I love sunshine. I value being outdoors! I value health! I get excited about working out all the time. I have truly made the leap into health the last five years. Before that, I valued it, yet I wasn't doing it. I encourage you not to make the same mistake I did. I like helping people win. That's important to me. Wisdom is one of my values.

Now, what about you? What are the issues you truly believe in? What do you like to talk about?

## Exercise: Values Tournament

Now I'm going to give you an example of what I do when people come to my studio. I have a deck of cards that lists sixty different values. I've listed those sixty values for you below, and I would like to invite you to sit down and go through them and select your top twenty values by numbering them in the spaces to the side. Now, out of those twenty, select your top ten. That doesn't mean you don't value the other things; you're just choosing the ten that mean the most to you.

Here are the sixty values:

| | | |
|---|---|---|
| _____ Affection | _____ Friendship | _____ Personal Brand |
| _____ Alignment | _____ Fun | _____ Personal Improvement |
| _____ Altruism | _____ Generosity | _____ Personal Salvation |
| _____ Appearance | _____ Genuineness | _____ Philanthropy |
| _____ Appreciated | _____ Happiness | _____ Power |
| _____ Attitude | _____ Harmony | _____ Productivity |
| _____ Cleanliness | _____ Health | _____ Recognition |
| _____ Congruence | _____ Honesty | _____ Respect |
| _____ Contentment | _____ Humility | _____ Results |
| _____ Cooperation | _____ Inner Peace | _____ Romance |
| _____ Creativity | _____ Inspiration | _____ Routine |
| _____ Education | _____ Intimacy | _____ Security |
| _____ Effectiveness | _____ Joy | _____ See the World |
| _____ Efficiency | _____ Knowledge | _____ Simplicity |
| _____ Fairness | _____ Lifestyle | _____ Solitude |
| _____ Faith | _____ Loved | _____ Spiritual Maturity |
| _____ Fame | _____ Loyalty | _____ Status |
| _____ Family | _____ Motivation | _____ Wealth |
| _____ Financial Security | _____ Openness | _____ Winning |
| _____ Freedom | _____ Organization | _____ Wisdom |

Now, list your top ten values on a separate sheet of paper, get your phone out, and take a picture of it. Save that picture. Post it. Share it with your spouse, if you're married, and with your kids. Share it with your partners. Put your values on your computer. Put them everywhere. Those are the ten primary values that you want to build your goals from and that you want to build your life from.

**BUILD YOUR GOALS AND YOUR LIFE FROM YOUR PRIMARY VALUES.**

So here's the question: How many times have you felt unmotivated when it comes to setting goals and staying true to your plan? Well, part of that is possibly because you haven't had clarity on your values; you haven't truly understood what your values are. Understanding what is important to you can be a big motivator. For many people, including me and probably you, our motivation fluctuates up and down. If you have clarity on your values, you can have a much more powerful life in terms of both your motivation and the decisions you make.

You want to avoid friction by not chasing after goals that aren't in alignment with your values. For example, let's say you want to make a ton of money, whatever that amount is, and you work very hard and make that money. However, if one of your top values is health, and you never take the time to be healthy because you're working so hard to make money, guess what? You're not living a life that's congruent with your values. You're not going to end up with the results you want. That's what I was doing; I got fat. It was embarrassing when I looked at myself and realized that I was forty or fifty pounds overweight. I thought, *Here I am preaching to others, and I'm not living it.* So I just stepped back and said, *You know what? I need to keep adjusting my schedule. I need to figure out how my body works. I need to eat differently to be able to live in alignment with my values.* And that may be true for you, as well.

If the goals we're setting are not congruent with our values, it can cause an internal conflict that compromises our results. It can stress us out and keep us up at night. We need to make sure we have that clarity.

When our goals are out of alignment with our values, it's like riding in a car with tires that are out of alignment—it's a bumpy ride.

Values clarification is an important piece to the puzzle of high achievement. It's certainly a building block upon the exceptional life we all want to live.

A few years ago my family and I were on a skiing vacation in the mountains, and I took my deck of values cards with me. Our plane was delayed about an hour; so I sat down with my kids and laid those cards out, and we helped each other get clear on our values. Imagine doing that with your kids. How valuable would that be, to help them understand at a young age where they're going?

> VALUES CLARIFICATION IS AN IMPORTANT PIECE TO THE PUZZLE OF HIGH ACHIEVEMENT.

After you define your values, you may need to adjust and reprioritize your goals. We're going to get into that in the next section, where I'm going to show you how to build a vision board that will help you link your values to your goals.

## GOAL SETTING

Now we're on one of my favorite subjects of all times: goal setting.

From the time I was seventeen, as a young entrepreneur, I started writing down my goals. In fact, the first goal I wrote was to become a millionaire by the time I was twenty-five. I typed it up on an old typewriter (it was that long ago), framed it, and put it on the wall in my room—and I became a millionaire two years before my target date! Understanding the power of goal setting is something I love to impart to people, and I am going to do that for you right now.

In this section, we're going to cover all of the pieces that relate to goal setting, and I want to encourage you to pull out your phone. We're going to be talking about putting your goals everywhere, and that includes on your phone. Put them anywhere you will see them every day. I have a big vision board in my garage, so when I pull into my garage I can see my goals. I encourage you to do the same.

Why is that important? I believe so strongly in goal setting that I take it to the highest level. For example, let me tell you about my gym. When I am between sets while I'm working out in my gym, I watch videos that I've created with inspirational sayings on them. I put flip charts in my gym, so while my trainers are teaching me things, we're setting goals for what we want to accomplish. I have my health goals on my wall, so I can see where I've been and where I'm going as I am working out. I have etched into my mirror who I want to become.

> SHOW ME A PERSON WHO DOESN'T SET GOALS, AND I'LL SHOW YOU A PERSON WHO DOESN'T HAVE A VERY RICH LIFE.

As you can tell, I am into goal setting in a big way, and I hope that's where you're headed, too. If you want to have extraordinary results, you have to take this one seriously.

**Show me a person who doesn't set goals, and I'll show you a person who doesn't have a very rich life.** You have to know where you're going. When you create a vision, you have to set up a plan to achieve it, and you have to have a clear understanding when you're putting all those pieces together.

*Inc.* magazine recently came out with an article that lists six things that the most successful companies have in common. Number one on the list was setting goals—even before things like choosing the right markets, raising capital, building the team, gaining share, and adapting to change! From a business perspective as well as from a personal perspective, goal setting is so important!

In fact my good friend, the late Zig Ziglar, said, "You need a plan to build a house. To build a life it is even more important to have a plan or goal." How about you? Do you have a plan with good goals to get you there? Can you imagine contracting for someone to build a house for you without a plan? Do you think that house would even closely resemble what you had in mind? Probably not, right? If you want to have an extraordinary life, you have to have an extraordinary plan.

Think about the rest of your life and what you would like to accomplish. Where will you be in five years? Ten years? Thirty years? When you're eighty, where will you live, how healthy do you plan to be, and how will you spend your free time? As you remember from earlier, to gain the kind of clarity required for you to get extraordinary results faster, you must know two things: your current conditions and your vision of where you want to be. Between these two points is a gap that must be bridged by your actions. These actions also can be described as goals. Goals create a variety of activities designed to produce predictable results and success. Pursuing goals takes you from where you are now to where you want to be.

> IF YOU WANT TO HAVE AN EXTRAORDINARY LIFE, YOU HAVE TO HAVE AN EXTRAORDINARY PLAN.

Let me share with you a quote I say often: "We don't miss what we haven't imagined." That's why we write down our goals; they work for us when they become tangible. When we write them down, it allows us to visualize and take ownership of what we want, and it helps us get organized. Our written goals provide clarity, and they help us filter out activities that don't lead to results.

In 2007, Dr. Gail Matthews of Dominican University of California's Department of Psychology conducted a study of how we influence goal achievement when we write our goals down. She asked 149 participants from businesses, organizations, and networking groups in the United States and overseas to set goals either by (1) thinking about them, (2) writing them down, (3) writing down their goals and the actions they committed to in order to accomplish them, (4) writing down their goals and their action commitments and sharing both with a friend, and (5) writing their goals and action commitments and sending weekly progress reports to a friend.

At the end of four weeks, only 43 percent of Group 1 (those who only thought about their goals) had made any significant progress.

However, Group 2 (those who had written their goals) did 42 percent better than Group 1. And more than 76 percent of the last group (who combined written goals, action commitments, and weekly progress reports sent to a friend) had attained their goals.[1]

Goals give us a blueprint or map for creating the life we envision and living by the values that are import-ant to us. Writing down and visualizing our goals activates our reticular activating system, or RAS, which is our brain's way of helping us reach our goals. We'll talk more about that later.

> GOALS GIVE US A BLUEPRINT OR MAP FOR CREATING THE LIFE WE ENVISION AND LIVING BY THE VALUES THAT ARE IMPORTANT TO US.

## VISION (RESULTS) BOARDING

Now I want to talk about vision boarding, because it is such an important concept in helping you reach your goals. In fact, I personally believe vision boarding has even more of an impact than anything else you can do, because it helps you mentally and emotionally link your vision to your goals and makes it come alive to you.

First, let me warn you: Don't be a squatter! I don't know if you've heard that term, so let me bring it to life for you. About fifteen years ago I had an impactful opening in my life to the idea of creating a vision board. Someone had shared the concept with me that you needed to tie your goals to your vision and that a vision board was an excellent way to link them together. I thought, *You know, it is a good idea to have a vision board.* You know what I did about it? Squat! I was a squatter, because I didn't do squat about it. I don't want you to be a squatter. I want you to be a doer!

So a year went by, and I heard about the concept again. Again I

---

1 Dr. Gail Matthews, "Goals Research Study," 2007, http://www.dominican.edu/academics/ahss/undergraduateprograms/psych/faculty/assets-gail-matthews/researchsummary2.pdf

thought, *That's a good idea!* And do you know what I said after about two or three more years? I finally said, *You know what? I am going to do it!* And it has had such a dramatic impact on my family and my life that I want to encourage you to do the same thing—build a board that says, "Who do you want to become? What do you want to share? What do you want to experience? And, of course, what do you want to have?"

Before we go into how to build a vision board (which is also called a results board), let's see how important a vision board is in helping our reticular activating system (RAS) do its job.

## RAS—Reticular Activating System

Many people don't set goals because they don't know about the RAS. At the bottom of your brain is a set of nerves that allows you to bring things into your brain that you need, want, or desire. If you have a goal, then that's something you're interested in, and your brain allows it to come in.

Have you ever bought a new car and all of a sudden you see that car everywhere you go? You think, *Wow! That car is everywhere!* And you wonder why you hadn't seen those cars before. The week before you bought the car, all those same cars were everywhere around you, and yet your brain wasn't aware that you were interested in that car.

This is the way the reticular activating system works:

SINCE THE RETICULAR ACTIVATING SYSTEM ALLOWS THINGS THAT YOU'RE INTERESTED IN TO COME INTO YOUR LIFE, WHEN YOU WRITE DOWN YOUR GOALS, THEY BECOME PART OF THE LAW OF ATTRACTION THAT ALLOWS WHAT YOU CARE ABOUT TO COME IN THROUGH YOUR RAS; AND THAT HAS A HUGE IMPACT ON HELPING YOU ACHIEVE THOSE GOALS.

Let's say you go into a room where there's a chandelier hanging from the ceiling. You are in the process of building your home, and you have been thinking about putting a chandelier in your dining room. So when you look up and see the chandelier in the room you're standing in, all of a sudden you're very interested and you look at all the distinctions. If you weren't building a house, you wouldn't be thinking about chandeliers; that chandelier would still be there, and yet your reticular activating system would not even care about it. Your brain probably wouldn't even let it in.

Since the reticular activating system allows things that you're interested in to come into your life, when you write down your goals, they become part of the law of attraction that allows what you care about to come in through your RAS; and that has a huge impact on helping you achieve those goals. You not only see the goals in your mind; you also begin to see things around you that will help you achieve your goals. If you don't write them down, then your brain is not as clear about their importance and your RAS filters out things you might need to help you achieve your goals.

## Three Keys to Leveraging the RAS

There are three keys to leveraging the RAS:

1. Writing down (or typing) your goals

2. Visualizing your goals

3. Employing congruent self-talk

At this point, you may be saying, "All right Tony, you have me. I am going to write my goals down. And I understand that visualization is an important piece of the puzzle." Don't just stop there, though. Make sure that what you're visualizing is congruent with what you write down, and then put your visualization pieces everywhere—in your bedroom, in your closet, on your phone, in your bathroom, and anywhere else you will see it every day.

The third piece of that is what many of people miss, and I don't want you to miss it: positive self-talk that is congruent with your goals.

For example, if your goal is to be organized and you say things like, "Well, you know, I am not a very organized person," then you have self-sabotaged. You need to be saying positive things like, "I'm getting more organized so I can reach my goals."

When you have all three of those actions working for you, it triggers your RAS to let things in that allow you to put more mental energy on the things you want.

Let me bring out another point here. So many people focus just on what they want to have, and that's only one piece of the puzzle. Your goals should include not only what you want to have; they should also include what you want to share, what you want to experience, what you want to give, and what you want to become. Having clearly defined goals allows you to literally design your own life.

> YOUR GOALS SHOULD INCLUDE NOT ONLY WHAT YOU WANT TO HAVE; THEY SHOULD ALSO INCLUDE WHAT YOU WANT TO SHARE, WHAT YOU WANT TO EXPERIENCE, WHAT YOU WANT TO GIVE, AND WHAT YOU WANT TO BECOME.

## RESULTS (VISION) BOARDING

Let's talk a little bit more about results boarding (which is also called vision boarding) and how you can make that happen once you have your goals written down. Results boarding is a very powerful tool.

You start by going to a store like Home Depot or Lowes and buying a stack of one-foot-square cork boards. They usually come in sets of thirty-two. Take them home and decide where you want to put your vision board so you can see it every day. Then just start putting up the squares. You can make it any size you want—one square, three by four, four by four, or even four by eight if you want a big one. And you can add to it as your goals grow

After you have the cork board up, type a sign to put at the top that says something like "Results Board" or "Goals Board." Then put pictures on the board of anyone who will be involved in your goals—if you're doing this for your team, put a picture of your team on there; if you're doing it for yourself, post a picture of yourself; and if it's a family vision board, put a picture of your family on there.

One of the powerful things that people often miss in goal setting is having a family mission statement. I encourage you to put your family mission statement right in the center of your goals board if you have a family or your personal mission statement if you don't. Then I encourage you to post a list of the values you just identified, because you want everything you visualize to be congruent with your values. Then start collecting pictures that represent your goals, pulling from magazines, your personal or family picture albums, or items you see on the Internet, and post them. Again, these pictures should represent what you want to have, what you want to become, what you want to share, what you want to experience, and what you want to give. Build your goals board out and look at it over and over and over again. And if you have a family, I encourage you to get your family involved in building your goals board so that you're all seeing it all the time.

**IF YOU WANT TO GET THE MOST OUT OF THIS BOOK, THEN MAKE SURE YOU'RE BUILDING YOUR VISION BOARD.**

You may be saying, "Building a goals board is a little weird." Well, it may be, and yet I'm telling you that it does work. Again, I encourage you not to be a squatter by not doing squat about your vision board now that you've heard how powerful the concept is. If you want to get the most out of this book, then make sure you're building your board. I believe there are no lazy people— only visionless people. Think about that one. Don't make the mistake of not imagining where you can go in your life. Lost time is never found again, so don't waste time. Just do it.

Now let's get into how to set and achieve your goals.

# Five Keys for Setting and Achieving Goals

1. **Pull from others!** Let me share a story with you. I got a call from my coach about thirteen years ago and he said, "Tony, I've met a guy who has more goals than you do," and I said, "Really?" "At the time I had fifty pages of goals. He said "Yes, this guy has more goals than you, and I can get you a copy of them." I said, "Fantastic! Get me a copy!"

So he did. The goals were in a binder, and I saw that, sure enough, this guy had seventy-five pages of goals to my fifty. I thought that was cool. As I looked through the binder I saw that his goals were actually congruent with my values, so I thought, *Why don't I just take some of his goals?* So I took about fifty pages of his goals and added them to my fifty pages; and now I had one hundred pages, which was more than he had. Right?

Spin forward about eleven years, when I got an e-mail from this guy! His name is Peter Thomas. He said, "Tony, *Strategic Acceleration* is the best book I've ever read. I want to buy one hundred of them! I need to pass these out to all of my friends." Now, he didn't know that I had been living his goals for eleven years and that part of the book was tied to him!

Then he said, "I've read all your websites. Man, we think quite a bit alike!" Since then, we've become friends. In fact, I've become his coach, and I'll tell you more of that story a little bit later in the book. Just know this: This guy is one of the highest achievers I've ever met in my life, and he is into goal setting in a big way, just like I am, and just like I'm encouraging you to be.

2. **Write down one hundred things.** One of the simplest ways to get started is to write down one hundred things you want to achieve. I started doing this in 1986, and at that time I could only get to sixty-two! When I suggest to other people that they do this, many of them get stuck at thirty! So I am going to challenge you to see if you can list one hundred things you truly want to achieve in your life while you're living on this earth.

One of the items I wrote down in 1986 was that I wanted to play the piano. The year 1987 went by, and I hadn't made any impact on achieving this particular goal. Then 1988 went by, then 1990. Fast forward to 1995. One day I was walking through a shopping mall and I heard a piano playing. I looked over and saw a beautiful grand piano—and it was playing by itself! That was the first time I had ever seen that. Then I saw that the words of the song the piano was playing were displayed in digital format. I thought, *This is cool. If I bought one of those I could get a remote control, and I could play the piano.*

So I took my wife over to the piano warehouse, and I walked in and said, "I want to buy one of those pianos." When the guy quoted me a gigantic price, all I could say was, "Wow!" So he said, "Well, what's your budget?" and I quoted him a much smaller number. He said, "Sorry. You won't get a piano like this for that amount."

So I thought, *I know what I'll do. I'm going to put out the word that I want a grand piano.* I did just that, and my dad called me a few weeks later and said, "There's a grand piano for sale in the estate of the people who used to live across the street from me, and you can buy it for three grand." So I bought this beautiful grand piano and had it shipped to the piano warehouse. I paid them to put all of the necessary electronics on it, and I ended up having a lovely grand piano in my home, where I can hit the button on my remote and play the piano.

How about you? Are you creative in your goal setting? Start writing down your one hundred things, and let life come in and help you make it happen.

3. **Write down your accomplishments!** Many people fail to do this. Maybe you accomplished things in high school, such as in sports, or maybe you accomplished some exceptional things in college. Or you may have traveled to certain places that you truly wanted to go to. Writing down your accomplishments—what you've seen, done, or experienced—can have a huge inspirational impact on you as you're setting more goals.

4. **Write down your goals in each of your top values**. Take your top values and write down at least one goal that ties to each value.

5. **Document a perfect day, week, or month—or maybe all three!** What would that look like for you? Think about it and then write it down.

## STORY: BRIAN TRACY

Let me give you one more piece of advice, which has to do with something Brian Tracy told me. I've followed Brian and watched his videos for years, and I ended up becoming friends with him. He's a super nice guy! I was having lunch with him one day a few years back, and we were talking about goal setting. (Remember when I was talking about thinking, I said I like to tap into people's brains, so I like to hang around cool people.) I asked his opinion about some of the goals I'd written down that I wasn't accomplishing, and he said to me, "Tony, are those still your goals?" I said, "Not really!" He said, "Well, then change them!" My thinking had been—because this principle was on my belief window—that I had written them down, so I needed to go get them. I said that to him, and he said, "No, you can change!" That was such a powerful and liberating thought to me! I say the same thing to you today. Maybe you need to update your goals. If you have goals written down today that change two or three years from now, that's okay. Change them! It's your life.

> **KEEP YOUR GOALS IN FRONT OF YOU AT ALL TIMES, BECAUSE VISUALIZATION HAS A POWERFUL EFFECT ON YOUR TRANSFORMATION.**

The information I've shared with you in this chapter is powerful, and it will change your life. Decide what wealth looks like to you. What is your purpose? What makes you happy? What are you passionate about? Use those answers to help you define your values, and then set goals that are congruent with those values. Keep your goals in front of you at all times, because visualization has a powerful effect on your transformation. It drives your desires and produces the voluntary change that will help you achieve results faster.

Now let's delve into the second piece of the *Strategic Acceleration* formula: Focus!

# V.I.P.s

- Wealth—we all want it, and it's much more than money. It's living on purpose and spending time doing what makes you happy and/ or what you're truly passionate about.

- You are the architect. You can design the life you want. When you come to a crossroads in your life, you have to define with clarity what you want to have.

- Whether it's business or just you, having clearly defined values that align with your goals and vision for the future is a must.

- If you have clarity on your values, you can have a much more powerful life in terms of both your motivation and the decisions you make.

- Goals need to be written, visualized, and mentally owned. Make sure you get that, and then you can actually design your own life.

- Goals give us a blueprint or map for creating the life we envision and living by the values that are important to us.

# CHAPTER 3:

# FOCUS

To get results that will take you to the next level, you must master the second step in the three-step formula: Focus. Focus will help you identify and concentrate on what matters the most for the success of your vision, and it will help you filter out distractions that hinder its progress.

Getting superior results faster is critical to your success. Focus is a huge piece to the puzzle for getting results in an accelerated time-frame, and I know that's what you want. **Focus is the opposite of distraction, and it is crucial for every high achiever.** It takes an intentionally focused person to minimize distractions.

This is the single most impactful area that provides the greatest opportunity for improvement for the majority of the people I fine-tune, support, and advise. Our hectic speed of life makes it easy to get sidetracked. People lose focus and often don't even realize it until they or their organizations begin to suffer. Often, the difference between someone who is successful and someone who isn't is focus. You truly do get more of what you focus on.

Many leaders operate in overwhelm mode. They get mired in their daily activities, unable to get off the hamster wheel of meeting after meeting. In fact, I ask many of my executives, "What percentage of your time do you spend in meetings?" You may be as surprised as I was at the answer most give (or, then again, your answer may be the same): They spend 50 to 70 percent of their time in meetings! The unfortunate thing is, many times they shouldn't even be in the meetings they attend, because that means they aren't focused on the important things they need to be doing to move their organizations forward. They're covered up with meetings, e-mails, calls, and activities, and those things shouldn't be their real focus. In this chapter, I'm going to show you how to zero in on the activities that will get you the results you want.

> SUCCESS TRULY HINGES ON THE ABILITY TO CUT THROUGH THE CLUTTER, DROWN OUT THE NOISE, AND FOCUS ON THE HIGH LEVERAGE ACTIVITIES THAT ARE THE BACKBONE OF REACHING YOUR VISION.

Focus is not something that comes naturally for most people. It's a skill that must be learned, polished, and practiced. It is mental discipline—the thinking skill required to get the results you want. Success truly hinges on the ability to cut through the clutter, drown out the noise, and focus on the *High Leverage Activities* that are the backbone of reaching your vision.

There's just one problem: it's extremely easy to get distracted! If you don't have focus, the pull created by clarity goes down, and you're much less likely to achieve what you want in life. On the other hand, when you consciously work to develop the ability to focus strategically, then the pulling power of clarity will be enhanced, and you'll be able to execute effectively. You'll get the results you want faster.

Have you ever watched a college or a professional basketball game when it's very close and one of the players on the away team gets fouled? As this guy is standing, looking at the basket and getting ready to take his free-throw shot, thousands of fans all around him are screaming. Cheerleaders are waving their pom-poms, and everyone is doing whatever they can to distract him and stop him from sinking the shot. He has to block out all of that mayhem and focus only on getting the ball in the basket. It's amazing that anyone can do that! Professional athletes in every sport are fanatical about practicing their focusing skills because they know their results depend upon it. The difference between someone who's successful and someone who isn't is often the ability to focus intently on the object or goal.

If you're like many people, you don't realize the real extent of your distractions. If you want to get serious about focusing to improve your results, I encourage you to keep a Focus Journal for two weeks. Every day write down your priorities and tasks for the day, and then keep a log of the time you spent focused on them. Also keep track of each distraction and how long it pulls you away from what you intended to do. When you review the Journal, you may be very surprised at how much of your time is spent on distractions. This one exercise will give you a great deal of clarity about where your focus needs to improve!

I've developed some very powerful tools to help my clients, and now you, improve their focus. They are: MOLO (More Of, Less Of), *High Leverage Activities*, and saying "no."

MOLO is a very powerful—and yet very simple—activity that can literally change your life. It's basically eliminating activities you shouldn't be doing. First, you want to determine what you want more of and what you want less of, and then you need to determine what you need to do more of and what you need to do less of in order to get there. I'm going to bring that to life for you.

The second lesson we're going to talk about is the core—the biggest foundational piece of the entire course—and that is *High Leverage Activities*. I'm going to show you how to identify them, how to document them, and how to design them in both areas of your life (personal and professional).

Then we'll look at another huge piece to staying focused: Saying "no." Saying "no" often and effectively is another overlooked secret. Some of the most successful people who have ever lived have said this one single action is absolutely necessary for success. In fact, if you truly want better results, you have to get this one down.

# MOLO

In business, an audit is designed to show you the assets and liabilities you currently have, right? The goal of an audit is to help you create a better allocation of your time, effort, and resources so you can get greater returns and greater results. That's what a MOLO can do. It can show you where you're wasting your efforts, often in small ways. Also, it also can help you get clear on where you should be spending your time to get more "bang for your buck," so to speak, so you can significantly move the results needle.

To introduce the concept of MOLO (More Of, Less Of), let me tell you a story about a friend of mine I talked a little about earlier. His name is Peter Thomas, and he was the co-author of a wonderful book we did together called *Business Ground Rules*, in which we identified one hundred things every entrepreneur should do.

You may remember the part of the story I told earlier: Peter sent me an e-mail and said, "Tony, I want one hundred of your *Strategic Acceleration* books." He had looked at all of my websites, and he said, "Man, you think quite a bit like me!" Now remember, I had been living this guy's goals for eleven years, and he didn't even know it.

Well, here's the rest of the story: In his e-mail he said, "I want us to have a relationship, and I might like to write a book with you. Why don't you give me a call?" So three hours later I gave him a call. Five minutes into the call he said, "Wait a second! I want to get my wife on the line." So he got his wife Rita on the line, and the three of us talked for three hours! He invited me to go up to Vancouver and visit with him on his yacht to talk about our relationship. So Tammy and I flew up, and I had been on his yacht for one hour when he said, "Dude, I want to hire you to be my coach for life!" I said, "You're on!" Well, I don't think he actually realized who he was talking to. I said "Peter, let me tell you. I brought my writer with me, and we're going to write this book." He was impressed.

Now Peter had co-founded Entrepreneurs' Organization (EO) all the way back in 1987. (EO is a global, peer-to-peer network of more than 11,000 influential business owners across the globe; in fact, it has 157 chapters in 48 countries.) He took Century 21 and built it into a giant franchise all across Canada. He built the Four Seasons Resort in Scottsdale, Arizona. He's an amazing serial entrepreneur who has done more in the last four decades than I can even list, including developing billions of dollars in real estate projects like shopping centers, apartments, condominiums, and golf courses.

After we wrote the book, another good friend of mine, Jay Rodgers, who is also my mentor, jumped into the story. Jay was nice enough to co-sponsor a launch party at the Dallas Country Club with the local Dallas EO Chapter, where Peter and I launched our book. Peter was the keynote speaker at the party, and one of the things he talked about was how impactful MOLO has been for him. In the RESULTS Faster! online course that corresponds with this book, we show a clip of that speech, and I invite you click on this link to watch it now: **https://www.youtube.com/watch?v=59aWucBXks8. It's an incredible endorsement from a guy who truly believes in MOLO.**

Years ago I wrote a book called *How to Gain 100 Extra Minutes a Day*. Over time, that book has been condensed into the MOLO concept. MOLO allows you to make a better investment of time.

## MORE OF

We've developed a template for the MOLO matrix and will be happy to share it with you. Just email us at tonyjeary.com to request a copy. Or you can easily duplicate it on a sheet of paper by simply making two columns. In the first column, list these two categories:

• More Of
• Less Of

In the second column list the corresponding activities that apply to each area. Next to the "More Of" column, list what you need to start doing more of to get the results you want. These are the actions that will move the results needle. It could be something like creating daily lists. Maybe you're doing that sometimes, and yet you need to do more of it. Or maybe you need to prioritize your lists more, or you need to build more tools, or perhaps you need to purchase more updated tools. Or maybe you want more new clients.

## LESS OF

Next to the "Less Of" column, list things you need to thin down and get out of your life. Sometimes you need less clutter. So how would you deal with that? Well, think about it. People may give you quite a few gifts, and maybe you buy a ton of gadgets. Over the years, you've accumulated all this "stuff," and when you look around you see plenty of clutter. Clutter is something you need less of. Just get rid of it. Another example of something you need less of is ineffective meetings! Everyone wants less of that.

**FINDING OUT WHAT YOU TRULY WANT MORE OF AND WHAT YOU WANT LESS OF IS AN IMPORTANT STRATEGIC LIFE MOVE.**

Making a list of what you want more of and less of is extremely impactful in maximizing your time. You can do this not only for your personal life, but for your professional life, as well; in fact, you should do both. And you can do a MOLO for your family or for your team. You can even do a MOLO for your board! In just a few weeks we'll be bringing the board of a company I'm working with into my studio, and I'm going to be pushing them, as a group of six people who run the company, to identify what they want more of and what they want less of.

MOLO can actually be an audit of your life, per se, and it's an interesting concept. Finding out what you truly want more of and what you want less of is an important strategic life move. I believe you'll find it refreshing.

Why don't you start right now by doing a MOLO exercise of your vision and goals, since you want to have these clearly in your mind? Let me walk you through it.

Step 1: More of. What do you need to do more of to make your vision and goals a reality? Put at least three things you should do more of, and why. (This can be for either your personal or professional life.)

Step 2: Less Of. Now, what do you need to do less of so you can achieve your vision and goals? What should you eliminate, reduce, or let go of—and why? Come up with at least three things you need to do less of or let go of entirely.

Step 3: Start Doing. What do you need to start doing so you can realize your vision and goals faster? Do you need to be more organized and disciplined? Do you need to start taking courses so you can put in for a promotion or get a new job? Do you need to pay better attention to your spouse or your kids? What do you need to start doing, and why?

Step 4: Stop Doing. What do you need to stop doing, and why? There are some activities you may need to cut down on, like checking e-mail too frequently or getting rid of clutter in your home or office. And there are some things you may just plain need to stop doing completely. Procrastinating. Blaming other people. Holding inefficient, unnecessary meetings. Making excuses for not doing the things that will move you closer to your vision, values, and goals. In Step 4 you have to be honest with yourself. Are there bad habits you need to get rid of right now? Why is it so important to get rid of them? If you have more than one, be honest enough to say so, and then get rid of those activities or habits.

IF YOU'RE GOING TO MAKE THE INVESTMENT IN DOING A MOLO AUDIT, MAKE SURE YOU'RE ALSO GOING TO INVEST THE TIME AND TAKE THE ACTION THAT YOU SAY YOU'RE GOING TO TAKE.

Now, if you're going to make the investment in doing a MOLO Audit, make sure you're also going to invest the time and take the action that you say you're going to take. A MOLO Audit is a fantastic focusing tool, and yet you have to execute—you have to do what you wrote down. When you start using the principle of MOLO to focus your efforts, it'll increase your effectiveness immensely. It'll also give you more time and energy to put toward those activities that provide the most leverage in your life and business.

If you want to go even deeper, let me encourage you to use MOLO for your health—and I am talking about closely looking at what you should be doing more or less of, health-wise. Something you may want more of, for example, may be more intentionality in shopping for what you keep in your refrigerator or your health closet, or even in your pantry. Maybe you want more good vitals from your testing. What do you want less of? Maybe it's fat, or maybe it's less stress. It's so important to use MOLO so you can have real clarity in regard to your health.

Let me share something with you that we've done in my company. We got so clear with MOLO that we were able to adopt a mnemonic for the type of client we want to serve: ADOME.

**A**—Aggressive, appreciative and abundance thinking. We want clients who are able to make decisions as we drive their *Strategic Acceleration*, and we want them to appreciate how we positively impact their businesses and their lives. And we want our clients to want to openly share in the more that we create.

**D**—Desire to do business with us. We want people coming here saying, "Yes, we get who you are, and we want you to help us!"

**O**—Open-minded. Occasionally we have people who come in with their arms folded, and I say, "Do I need to talk you into working with me? I've been doing this for over thirty years. I have the best practice in the world, and if you come in here open-minded, I can pour into you and your results will take off." We want open-minded people who are ready for that.

**M**—Millions to be made. We prefer to work with people in the studio where there are millions of dollars at stake; we can help them make more money.

<u>E</u>—Equity play. We like to have the opportunity for some kind of success fee—maybe participating in part of the ownership or the growth based on the results we help them achieve.

## MOLO: Be a river, not a reservoir.

We want more ADOME clients and less of those who don't fit that profile. How about you? Why don't you MOLO your clients and see if the ADOME profile will work for you?

MOLO works for everything. Some people post their MOLO lists in a visible place in their home or office so they can keep MOLO top of mind.

My mom always says, "Be a river, not a reservoir," and I think the MOLO concept applies here. We need to get things out of our lives by letting them flow through our river and move on, and not let everything jam up the flow and make us into a reservoir.

Now, as we continue to experience the power of Focus, let's move on to *High Leverage Activities.*

# HIGH LEVERAGE ACTIVITIES (HLAs)

In Chapter 1 I told you about the two biggest takeaways from this book, the first of which was High Leverage Activities. *No single skill or habit has a more powerful impact on results than the ability to eliminate distractions and focus on your* **High Leverage Activities.**

When we wrote the *Strategic Acceleration* book I've been talking about, we didn't realize that the number one concept would be *High Leverage Activities* until we started getting feedback about the book from top achievers all over the world. As a result, we decided to write another book that just focused on HLAs. That book is called *Leverage,* and I'm going to bring that to life for you right now.

Leveraging your time is so valuable. Success is a results contest, and achieving superior results is based upon eliminating distractions that plague your daily time. You have to be able to spend your time on what matters most. We'll talk about that concept in this section, and then I'll share ways to eliminate distractions. I'll even give you some of my personal HLAs to help you better understand the concept.

We've divided this section into three parts: activities, distractions, and defining your HLAs.

## ACTIVITIES

Leverage is the ability to influence something in a way that multiplies the outcome of the efforts without a corresponding increase in the consumption of resources. It makes sense, then, that you should be doing *High Leverage Activities* (HLAs) about 70 percent of your time. Here's how that works: There are 168 hours in a week. We sleep for about fifty-six hours (or we should)—eight hours a day, fifty-six hours a week. Then we use about twelve hours (in round numbers) for maintenance. Subtract the fifty-six and twelve hours from 168, and that leaves you with about one hundred hours to spend. Generally speaking, we spend about fifty hours a week in our personal lives and about fifty hours in our professional lives. What I'm suggesting here is that we should think about and identify those HLAs that will have the most impact on our results, both personally and professionally, and focus 70 percent of our time in both areas on those HLAs. That means that we should spend roughly thirty-five hours of our professional time and about thirty-five hours of our personal time on the predetermined activities that will get us the best results.

Some examples of *High Leverage Activities* might be coaching and nourishing your team members, impacting those you serve, planning your day, and sharpening your skills. Be aware, though, that there are *Low Leverage Activities* (LLAs) that steal your time, such as wasted meeting time, doing activities that subordinates should be doing, and chasing down things you need because you are unorganized. You have to get more organized and get rid of those LLAs.

It's very important to calculate out how you spend your time. In general, what percentage of your time do you spend in *High Leverage Activities*, and what percentage of your time do you spend in *Low Leverage Activities*? Take just a moment to answer that question. Think about how much of your time you spend doing the things that truly matter the most, and then think of all of the things you do that waste many of your minutes each day. I'll bet you can see areas where you definitely need to improve, right?

## DISTRACTIONS

Distractions are a big part of everyday life. We all fight it. In fact, most people are burning five, ten, fifteen, twenty hours a week on things they shouldn't be doing—such as unnecessary paperwork and prolonged telephone calls. You could be zooming in on the time you spend on phone calls by saying right at the beginning something like, "Hey, I have about eight or ten minutes for this call," and then it becomes an eight- or ten-minute call instead of a twenty-five-minute call, and you're not distracted by wasting another fifteen minutes.

I went to the bank one day; and since my builder's office is in the same building as my bank, I thought I would see if I could do two things at once (I call that an *Elegant Solution*). So I called my builder and said, "Bailey, may I stop by and say hi? I need about seven minutes of your time."

So I stopped by his office and showed him a couple of things. Then, seven minutes after I had walked in, I said, "Hey, I have to go!" As I started to walk out the door, he said, "Hey, wait! I have more time," and I said, "I don't!" By doing that I was able to show him the value I put on my time, and it shaped the rest of our relationship because he knew that I make sure every minute counts.

If you don't want distractions in your life, you have to set up your boundaries. Most burn one to two hours a day because of poor e-mail management, when we should be burning about half of that on e-mails. **This is such an important topic that we made a bonus module for the *RESULTS Faster*! online course that that gives my best ideas on e-mails.** I've invested years studying and learning about the best way to

> IF YOU DON'T WANT DISTRACTIONS IN YOUR LIFE, YOU HAVE TO SET UP YOUR BOUNDARIES.

handle e-mails, and I have included ten proven concepts in the bonus module that you will love.

The same goes for meetings. They can be a huge distraction, because there is so much wasted time in meetings. So we've also done a bonus module on meetings that will give you a ton of powerful proven ideas to deploy.

## KEYS TO ELIMINATING DISTRACTIONS

Let me give you my four keys to eliminating distractions:

1. **Make good daily lists.** One thing we do in my organization is make a daily master list. We accumulate all the core things that need to happen each day and put them on one list, and then we huddle each morning and disseminate those out to five, six, or seven team members. We do that every day, so each person will have his or her focus for the day. At the end of the day we come back and see how we did on the things we needed to get done.

2. **Be organized to the max.** One of my ten professional standards is to have everything organized. When people come to work for me, I tell them right up front that this is one of my ten standards. I say to them, "If you can't live up to this, don't come to work for me. I want everything organized all the time—not just on Thursdays or every other day—because I don't want to be chasing things down. That means if we take books off the bookshelves, we replenish the supply right away. Everything is organized, because I don't want to waste time."

3. **Schedule your time on your calendar!** What does that mean? It means you have to learn to say "no" to certain things; you have to own your calendar. I can't emphasize this enough. We'll talk more about this in the next section. Saying "no" is not always easy, and I'll be sharing with you some killer ideas that will help you.

4. **Constantly audit yourself.** That means at the end of the day you say, "How did I do? Was I actually productive, or did I just do a ton of activities?" You have to be very serious about this if you

want to go to the highest level of eliminating distractions and get focused on the things you should be doing. Activities don't count! Productivity does! If you want to have extraordinary results, you have to manage that.

ACTIVITIES DON'T COUNT! PRODUCTIVITY DOES!

## DEFINING YOUR HLAS

We've talked about activities (*High Leverage* vs. *Low Leverage*) and how to eliminate distractions. Now the third—and foundational—piece of this section is defining your HLAs. It starts by knowing where you are and where you want to go. When you determine those two pieces of information, you'll see that there's a gap between them—and that gap should be filled with the HLAs you need to focus on in order to get you where you want to go.

Let me share with you my HLAs as examples, to help you better understand the concept.

These are my five HLAs on the personal side of my life:

1. Praying

2. Spending time with my wife

3. Spending time with my family

4. Doing things that are health related, including walking, exercising, eating right, and even relaxing and counting my blessings

5. Loving people. I love to encourage and nourish the people around me. That could include writing a note to someone, sending an e-mail, or making a phone call to my mom and loving on her.

So I should spend 70 percent of my fifty hours, or about thirty-five hours of my week, doing those things.

Now here are my five HLAs on the professional side:

1. Attracting strong, qualified business

2. Delivering great value. Hopefully you think that what I'm sharing with you in this book is powerful and that the time my team and I took to put it all together is of great value to you.

3. Clarifying the direction for my own operation. That's something I own, and perhaps you own it as well for your organization, whether it's small or large. We must clarify the direction and determine how to improve the operations.

4. Gaining wisdom. What does that mean for me? I am in the wisdom business, so that means I need to constantly be sharpening my wisdom. I need to be studying, reading, and documenting my business acumen so I have a strong arsenal of wisdom to share with people.

5. Nourishing my connections. I have a big Rolodex. That means I have a large number of contacts I need to nourish, so this is what I do: I autograph books every day, and I send many gifts to people. As a matter of fact, last Christmas I sent out 860 gifts. That's because I have quite a few people I want to nourish. I don't want to just take from them; I want to give to them, as well.

Those are the five things on my HLA list. If something comes into my life that doesn't fit into one of those categories, I have to weigh it very carefully before I say "yes" to it. This should be the same for you.

## HLA TOOL

Now I'd like to share with you my favorite tool for helping people I coach get clear on their HLAs. It's called an *Accelerator Matrix*. You can use this tool to help you determine both your personal HLAs and your professional HLAs; however, let's look at it from a professional standpoint.

---

# ACCELERATOR MATRIX

| # | HLAs / Focus Areas | Lead | Accelerators | Roadblocks to Bust |
|---|---|---|---|---|
| 1. | | | | |
| 2. | | | | |
| 3. | | | | |
| 4. | | | | |
| 5. | | | | |
| 6. | | | | |
| 7. | | | | |
| 8. | | | | |

Overall Objectives:

As an executive or a leader in your organization, you will need to determine what your professional HLAs are and then write them down on the left side of the matrix. One of them, for example, could be nourishing your people. Let's say you have twenty-five people in your organization and you have an executive assistant. In the "Lead" column, list your executive assistant as the one to lead the effort in helping you nourish your people. Now, what are some of the accelerators you can do to nourish your people? Maybe it's blocking out a ten-minute one-on-one connection with them each week, or maybe it's sending them an e-mail.

I recently suggested to one client who travels all over the world that his team send to him each Friday a list of what they accomplished that week; then a *High Leverage Activity* for him would to be look at those lists on Friday and respond to them. This would allow him to be constantly connected with them, and it would also fall under the *High Leverage Activity* of nourishing his people.

The last column is "Roadblocks." If your calendar gets so full with meetings that you're not able to nourish your people, that's a roadblock you have to avoid. You must do a better job of managing your calendar.

I encourage you to use this matrix, either for yourself or your organization, or both. It's a very simple yet powerful tool that will help you maximize your HLAs.

To summarize, you can get results faster by rooting out and getting rid of activities that drain you by making sure you have productivity and not just activity, by becoming more focused and avoiding your distractions, and by documenting your HLAs.

Now let's talk about something you have to do in order to be successful.

# SAYING "NO"

Are you saying "no" enough? In my opinion, that's the most important word there is in regard to productivity!

Saying "no" is an overlooked secret to success. I say this as an absolute—and I say it with conviction! In today's fast-paced world we're presented with opportunities almost every waking minute. There are commercials, messages, products, e-mails, phone calls, offers, meetings, and activities of all kinds bombarding us from all sides, and most people don't know how to deal with them effectively. They don't say "no" enough—and that probably includes you.

If you understand this one thing, you will be shocked at how much more time you will find in your day, week, and month. You'll have more choices to do what matters the most if you understand that you must say "no" to the things that don't matter. This is a magic rule; it takes discipline and good thinking to a whole new level.

**YOU'LL HAVE MORE CHOICES TO DO WHAT MATTERS THE MOST IF YOU UNDERSTAND THAT YOU MUST SAY "NO" TO THE THINGS THAT DON'T MATTER.**

Let me give you some powerful quotes from two very successful people that will bring this to life. Who has been probably the most impactful entrepreneur in America, and maybe in the world, in the last twenty-five years? If you're thinking Steve Jobs, you're correct. He changed the way the world listened to music. He changed the way movies are animated. He changed the way we compute. He changed the way we use a phone. He changed the way we think! And the guy who made such a huge impact on the world said this: **"It is only by saying 'no' that you can concentrate on the things that really are important."** I've studied Steve Jobs quite a bit, and when a guy who's had that much influence on so many people says something about how to be successful, we need to listen! Saying "no" actually does matter.

Now here's another one for you. Think, if you will, of an author that everyone who has been in business in the last twenty to twenty-five years is familiar with. In fact, he probably had as much or more impact than any other author within the business culture in that time frame. If the name that comes to mind is Stephen R. Covey, you're right again. I followed Stephen for many years. His book, *The 7 Habits of Highly Effective People*, sold over twenty million copies and had a huge influence on many people, including me. Here's what Stephen said about saying "no": **"You have to decide what your highest priorities are and have the courage to say 'no' to other things."** "No" is a powerful word.

## THREE REASONS PEOPLE DON'T SAY "NO"

If "no" is such a powerful word, why don't more people use it? There are three main reasons why people don't say "no."

1. They don't know how

2. They don't want to miss out on anything

3. They don't want to offend anyone

People pleasers are rarely wildly successful. I know—I fight it, too, because I like to please people just like you probably do. Saying "no" is important, and yet it doesn't have to be a negative. Saying "no" respectfully can be well received, and it will certainly help you do life better. If you don't learn how to say "no" to needless activities, things will pile up on your calendar and drain valuable moments, to say nothing of your energy, and will cause you to misconnect with your goals.

So many people say "yes" and get into messes or the wrong partnerships, deals, or relationships because they didn't say "no" at the right time. Most often the right time to say "no" is at the beginning. This applies personally, of course, as well as professionally.

I often say that making the power of "no" an accepted and expected part of a culture is an important priority for leaders. Talk with your team about the value of each person's time and assure them that saying "no" may be an appropriate response. Empowering your people (no matter where they are, or how big your team or organization is) to say "no" creates a realization among them that "no" is often the right answer, and they should not be offended when they hear it. Make the power of "no" an accepted and respected part of your personal and professional life. It is your overlooked secret to success!

How about you? If you lead a team or an organization of any size, do you teach your people to say "no" to the things that don't matter?

Let me give you an example that I hope you will always remember when you think of this concept of saying "no." Let's say that Roland calls me and says, "Hey, Tony, I was wondering if we could have lunch." So I think, *Roland wants to have lunch with me. Hmmm. Is that an HLA or not?* Then I think, *Well, maybe not.* Now, I like Roland. So I say, "What's up?" and Roland says, "Well, you know Juan, and I would like to meet Juan. I'd like to have lunch and talk about your making that connection." So I say, "Roland, how about this? I've known Juan for several years. What I can do is just send you both an e-mail to introduce you to each other, and instantly you guys can be connected. What do you think?" He says, "Great! I didn't have time to have lunch with you, anyway!"

**The point is that sometimes when people ask us to do something, we say "yes" without going deeper; we don't say "no" because we just haven't explored the issue enough to see if we can solve it without saying "yes" to what they want.** In the example I gave you, instead of burning two hours for lunch, I was able to give Roland what he wanted in a matter of seconds. So many people say "yes" to lunches and breakfasts and dinners when they shouldn't, because they don't go deep enough to see how they might connect with the objective or the potential in a faster way.

Now if you would enjoy having lunch with Roland, that's cool. I understand that; yet if you truly want to be on target about spending your time, you have to go a little deeper and understand the whole situation before you say "yes." People want to have lunch with me all the time, or they want to have a phone call or a meeting. They want to connect. And before I say "yes," I say "How about this? Let's start with a ten- or fifteen-minute phone call."

When I was coaching the president of Walmart, we would schedule phone calls on his calendar in five-minute increments! Now remember, he manages two million people. I was grateful to get those five-minute increments on his calendar!

I'm asking you to think about and truly understand this concept. HLAs matter! If it's not a *High Leverage Activity*, you have to ask yourself, "Should I say 'no'?" This principle is so powerful, and I want you to remember it forever!

## THE SECRETS TO SAYING "NO" SMARTLY

Handled incorrectly, a "no" can cause disastrous consequences. Handled properly, "no" can become a strategic habit. Learning when and how to say "no" is one of the most valuable lessons of leadership. Here are a few tips:

- "No" does not have to be a negative. Saying "no" respectfully is typically well received, and it will help you to own your life again.

- The first person we must learn to say "no" to is ourselves. We must say "no" to activities we would prefer to engage in, and "yes" to what we actually need to do.

- Most often the right time to say "no" is at the beginning. It's much harder to get yourself out of a commitment than to not make the commitment at all.

> HANDLED INCORRECTLY, A "NO" CAN CAUSE DISASTROUS CONSEQUENCES. HANDLED PROPERLY, "NO" CAN BECOME A STRATEGIC HABIT. LEARNING WHEN AND HOW TO SAY "NO" IS ONE OF THE MOST VALUABLE LESSONS OF LEADERSHIP.

- Don't be afraid to say "no" to *Low Leverage Activities*, even if you've been doing them for a while, so you can put more time toward your HLAs.

- Part of successfully saying "no" isn't about the word itself; it's about the intent behind it. Done properly, people will understand that you are saying "no" because their request doesn't fit into your strategic priorities. Your intent is to free yourself up to better prioritize your time to focus on your HLAs.

- Sometimes saying "no" actually means saying "not now." You may need to defer a meeting or a conversation until you've finished with other priorities, for example.

**THERE ARE MANY WAYS TO SAY "NO" AND MAKE PEOPLE FEEL THAT YOU STILL CARE.**

- There are many ways to say "no" and make people feel that you still care. You can say "no" to your child's request for an expensive gadget, for instance, and instead spend time teaching him or her a new sport or game. If you get invited to participate in a project that will pull you away from your HLAs, you can say "no" and suggest someone else for the job or give the project leader ideas and suggestions for getting things rolling.

The most important tip for saying "no" smartly is to make a habit of evaluating everything according to your HLAs. You should say "yes" very rarely, and only when the opportunity matches your priorities, and "no" to anything else.

As you can see, saying "no" is a key to focus. And focus is the key to reducing *Low Leverage Activities* and investing more in your *High Leverage Activities*. HLAs are an absolute requirement for achieving the right results faster. And no single habit has more impact on your ability to eliminate distractions than to focus on HLAs and say "no."

## FOUR CHARACTERISTICS OF FOCUSED THINKING

Let me close this chapter with four positive characteristics of focused thinking:

1. Fewer distractions, which comes from saying "no."

2. More *High Leverage Activities*, which comes from saying "no."

3. On-time performance, which comes from saying "no." (If you wonder why you're late sometimes, it's because you said "yes" to too much! Look at your calendar! Do you often miss deadlines because you have too much on it?)

4. Increased productivity, which comes from saying "no" often!

You have to get this down!

Let me give you one more quote. If I asked you, "Who is the richest guy in America from making smart investments," who would you say? It's Warren Buffett, right? And he is the richest guy because he's learned to say "no." Look at this extremely strong quote from him: **"The difference between successful people and really successful people is that really successful people say "no" to almost everything."** How about that? What's the guy worth—forty or fifty billion? The bottom line is, say "no" to things that don't matter so you can say "yes" to what does.

Now let's go on to the third and final leg of the *Strategic Acceleration* formula: Execution. Execution powerfully transitions Clarity and Focus into action so that expected results become a reality.

# V.I.P.s

- Know what you want more of, know what you want less of, know what you should do more of, and know what you should do less of.

- MOLO can actually be an audit of your life, per se. Finding out what you really want more of and what you want less of is an important strategic life move.

- Clearly defined HLAs are the secret to avoiding distractions and multiplying achievement, both personally and professionally.

- Activities don't count! Productivity does!

- Saying "no" smartly pays huge rewards!

- You'll have more choices to do what matters the most if you understand that you must say "no" to the things that don't matter.

## CHAPTER 4:

# EXECUTION

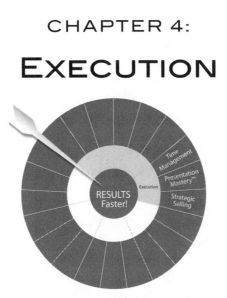

The third leg of the stool and the final part of the *Strategic Acceleration* formula is Execution. Once you've achieved clarity about where you want to go and get that pulling power working for you, you've identified your HLAs, and you've fine-tuned your focus, you have to take action. Execution is where the rubber meets the road. Understanding the execution process is much simpler once you've gained exceptional Clarity and determined your HLAs. Clarity and Focus, then, provide the roadmap for Execution.

## WHAT IS EXECUTION?

Execution is action at all levels. What does that mean? Good execution is getting things done. Great execution is getting things done fast and on purpose. And mastery execution is about getting the right things done and getting them done fast, on purpose, and with what I call *Elegant Solutions. Elegant Solutions* are those activities that allow you to accomplish multiple objectives with the same effort.

**You can create the greatest plan in the world and establish the most focused goals imaginable; yet if you fail to execute you're not going to achieve it. It's that simple.** The powerful thing about it is that the world pays for execution. Let me illustrate with a couple of stories.

One of my favorites is a true story from over one hundred years ago. When war broke out between Spain and the United States in the late 1890s, President McKinley needed to get an urgent message to General Garcia, who was somewhere in the mountains of Cuba, and no one knew where. Someone suggested to the president that a guy by the name of Rowan could find Garcia if anyone could.

Rowan was summoned to the president's office, and President McKinley said, "Can you get this message to General Garcia?" Rowan didn't ask why, he didn't ask how, nor did he ask any other questions. He just said "I will get it done, sir!" He took the message, put it in a pouch, put the pouch on a strap around his neck, and took off. He went to Cuba by boat, landed at night, and took off on foot through the hostile jungles of Cuba. When he came out on the other side of the island three weeks later, he had delivered the message to Garcia.

That true story was printed in an article by Elbert Hubbard in 1899. People loved it, and messages started pouring in. One message was from a guy in Chicago who owned an insurance organization, who said, "If you will print that story into a booklet, I'll buy 100,000 of them." It was printed, and the booklet became so popular so quickly that the little print shop that put it together couldn't handle the volume. They made arrangements for the guy in Chicago to print his own. Since that time, over forty million copies of this little booklet have been printed, and it has been translated into thirty-seven languages!

The real message of this story is that people love those who execute without asking a ton of questions and who don't get into the whys and why nots. They just take the assignment and go out and execute. Don't you love it when you have people working for you, or perhaps around you on your team, who just go out and execute? Don't you know bosses/customers/clients all love it when they ask you to do something and you go out and execute? The world flocks to people who get it done! **"Done" is one of my favorite words!** I love it when all the boxes on my team's master list are filled in with an "x."

Let me tell you another story, and this one is about me. In the early '90s I invested years in helping turn around Chrysler. The president of Ford heard about me, and I ended up personally coaching him. We built an exceptional relationship, and we had some amazing experiences. Then in the mid-nineties the top leaders at Ford said "Tony, we'd like to have you help us get the top two hundred or so of our executives together in a team building synergistic state." I said, "I'm not a team building expert." They said, "We'll pay you a million dollars," and I said, "I can become one!"

So I jumped in and started studying all of the distinctions about team building. Then I got to thinking, "Why would they give me a million dollars if I am not a team-building expert?" So I asked, and this is basically what they told me: "Because you get things done. We believe you can go out and learn it and make it happen." Think about that. Over twenty years ago they paid me a million dollars because I am someone who executes! The world really does flock to people who execute.

## THE WORLD FLOCKS TO PEOPLE WHO EXECUTE!

How about you? Do you get things done? Do you make it happen? I encourage you to think about that.

In the next three sections of this chapter, I'm going to really bring this out for you. We're going to be talking about managing time, and that includes prioritization, avoiding procrastination, improving your organization skills, and delegating more.

**Time is one of the most valuable commodities in the world; how we use it determines our success.** I am going to show you how to strategically answer the question throughout the day, *What's the best use of my time right now?* That's one of my favorite and most powerful time management secrets, and you'll find that I repeat it several times in different scenarios throughout this book.

We're also going to talk about *Presentation Mastery*™, which is one of my favorite subjects. In fact, I've authored over twenty-five books on the subject of presentation effectiveness, including my biggest best-seller, *Life Is a Series of Presentations.*

I was at a wedding a few months ago and I start getting texts from several of my friends. They were all saying, "Tony, you're on *Shark Tank!*" and I said, "No, I am at a wedding!" They said, "No, you're on *Shark Tank!*" and I repeated, "No, I am at a wed- 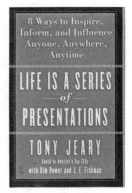 ding!" Well, I finally discovered that Daymond John of *Shark Tank* had recommended my book *Life Is a Series of Presentations* in an *Entrepreneur* magazine article. He said my book is one of the top six must-read books for anyone in business. I thought that was pretty cool. And guess what? I'm going to include highlights from *Life Is a Series of Presentations* in the section on *Presentation Mastery*™ in this chapter.

The next section is *Strategic Selling.* Until you know how to sell strategically, chances are you're not getting all the results you truly want. I want to help you determine who your stakeholders are, what they want, and how you get them to buy or take action where everyone wins. It's a very powerful section.

To achieve the right results faster, leaders must continually cascade their vision down through others in their organization so every team member understands and supports it. When you can persuade others to do the things you need them to do, you can make things happen and move the results needle. **The most successful people can effectively convince other people to take action on their behalf; therefore, they're able to execute at a high level.**

# Time Management

Time is an equalizer. We all have the same amount of time. No one has enough, yet everyone has all there is.

What you do with your time determines everything about your life. As we discussed in the last chapter, we all have 168 hours in a week. When you subtract the eight hours a day we should sleep (fifty-six hours a week) and the twelve hours for maintenance, that leaves us with one hundred hours. I want to talk to you in this chapter about how to strategically invest those one hundred hours. Everyone wants more time, and I am going to show you how to maximize your time by using four tools: prioritization, avoiding procrastination, organization, and delegation.

## PRIORITIZATION

Let me share with you eight keys to help you master the skill of prioritization:

1. **Set priorities that align with your predetermined HLAs, and review them throughout the day.** Eliminating unproductive tasks keeps you focused on the right things. To be time efficient, you must make sure your daily priorities align with your HLAs.

2. **Have strong written agendas.** Any meeting without an agenda—whether it's one you grant, one you attend, or one you lead—is often a huge time-waster. Think about what percentage of your time is wasted in meetings where there is no agenda and the meeting goes on forever in many different directions. Let me also note that many people don't understand the difference between objectives and agenda. They skip right to building an agenda. What should come first are the objectives you want to accomplish. A strong agenda will support the accomplishment of the meeting's objectives.

If someone wants you to attend a meeting, make sure there's a set of objectives and a written agenda. If not, then kindly guide the person who's calling the meeting in that direction by saying something like, "What do we want to accomplish here? Where are we going with this meeting? Are there two or three things we're going to cover?"

3. **Manage your high-energy times.** So many people miss this one. If you want to be at your peak performance and get things done right, you must manage your high-energy times. One way to do that is to know whether you are a morning person, or whether your peak energy time is mid-day or evening. Then schedule your impactful opportunities on your calendar according to your high-energy times.

Also understand that you can put yourself into high-energy states by playing music, by how you eat, by the people you're around, and by your environment. Make sure you make all that work for you so important minutes are managed to your advantage.

4. **Maximize your study.** For things like reading books or skimming articles and memos, commission team members or other colleagues to do your reading for you. My "need/want-to-read" book list gets pretty long. Does yours? A friend may call me and strongly recommend that I read certain books, and all I can think of is the length of my list. When you would really love to read all of the books recommended to you, and yet you know you just can't fit them all in with your HLAs, what do you do?

First, you prioritize them; then in the order of your priorities, maybe you can delegate the reading to a team member, friend, or even a college student, and have them summarize the book for you. Then you just read the summary. This is an excellent way to maximize your study and prioritize your time and focus.

How about magazine articles? Magazines are designed to seduce you into the advertisements. I suggest you first look at the Table of Contents and identify the articles you want to read; then prioritize the articles you selected, flag them by folding the selected pages, and go directly to the articles on those pages to maximize your study of each magazine.

5. **Put everything in bullets.** If you want to save time, put everything in bullets! Many people were taught growing up, like I was, to write long letters with paragraphs. Guess what? The real need for long letters and tons of paragraphs is pretty much nonexistent now. Generally speaking, bullets are the win. (This is not an absolute, of course.)

When you're going through and prioritizing your e-mail and you see one that has paragraph after paragraph, versus one that has everything in bullets, which one do you read first? The one with bullets, right? Remember to use bullets when you're sending e-mails, too.

6. **Do five-second huddles with yourself.** Before you make a phone

call, take five seconds and ask yourself, *What do I want to accomplish?* Then before you make the call, write down or at least think about your objective(s) for that call. So many times when we make a phone call and we get the person's voice mail, we don't have a clear objective in mind so we muddle through the message. If we're clear on our objective(s), we will leave better voice mails, which will expedite the results. It saves time on both ends.

7. **Delegate**. Ask the originators who send you e-mails, texts, voice mails, or any other type of communication to send you only relevant information. How many ccs and bccs do you get that you really don't need? Delegate those you don't, and then make sure you prioritize.

8. **List everything.** You will read this several times in this book. Lists are so important! Create, leverage, and review lists often; and as you're reviewing them, ask yourself my favorite little question, *What's the best use of my time right now?*

## PROCRASTINATION

When we launched *Strategic Acceleration* I also introduced the concept of positive and negative procrastination. I've since gone on to do a CBS special on the concept, and people are intrigued about it. Let me explain.

Think about your self-talk right now. Is it supporting you and giving you legitimate reasons to put things off or not? You see, all procrastination comes back to self-talk—what you say to yourself. Sometimes we say things like, *Oh, it doesn't really matter. I'll do that later. No one cares.* Or sometimes we may say, *You know, I just don't feel like doing that right now.* That's negative procrastination.

A legitimate thing to say to ourselves, when it's true, may be, *I need to take a little bit of time to gain some more valuable insights before I make that decision.* That's positive and *Strategic Procrastination.* Even if you say, *I need to sleep on it tonight,* because you know you'll make a better decision if you let your intuition work throughout the evening and night, that's positive procrastination.

Generally speaking, though, negative procrastination is putting things off when you shouldn't. To gain results, you need to take charge of your time and your life. Here are a few examples of possible ways to contradict negative self-talk.

- *I can do it tomorrow.* Ask, *What can I get started on now that will help me complete this project and help the others who are waiting for me?*

- *I don't have everything I need, so I'll wait.* Ask, *What can I do now, with what I have on hand?*

- *I can't do it perfectly (or, I need to do more research), so I'll wait.* See *"Production Before Perfection"* below in the four keys to dealing with procrastination.

- *I don't have time right now.* Ask, *What can I do in the next five (ten, fifteen, twenty) minutes that will move me toward the results I want?*

- *Someone else can do it better.* Say to yourself, *Even if someone else can do this better, it's my task and my responsibility. I may even get better as I keep working on this!*

- *I just don't feel like it right now.* Many people find that getting started is the biggest hurdle. Say to yourself, *I'll just do five (ten, fifteen, twenty) minutes of work on this.* You'll see that you often get caught up in the task and make tremendous progress.

Remember, it's only when you start doing what you need to do that you can begin to produce results. Waiting and *Strategic Acceleration* are not compatible. If you do nothing, that is exactly what you'll get—nothing. If you do something, the possibilities are endless. Be like Nike—Do it now!

Let's take a short assessment to see where you stand with procrastination. Rate yourself one to ten on these four questions, with one being often and ten being never.

1. How often do you push a task aside because you say to yourself you don't have enough time?

2. Do you find yourself often putting things off because of lack of clarity (you make things seem too complex)?

3. Are you often not productive or fast enough because you're too focused on perfection? (I know quite a few people, and that may include you, who fit into this category.)

4. How often do you let distractions (*Low Leverage Activities*) become a basis for your procrastination?

REMEMBER, IT'S ONLY WHEN YOU START DOING WHAT YOU NEED TO DO THAT YOU CAN BEGIN TO PRODUCE RESULTS. WAITING AND *STRATEGIC ACCELERATION* ARE NOT COMPATIBLE. IF YOU DO NOTHING, THAT IS EXACTLY WHAT YOU'LL GET—NOTHING. IF YOU DO SOMETHING, THE POSSIBILITIES ARE ENDLESS.

How did you do? If your score was on the low end, this could be one of the most valuable lessons in this book for you! I'm going to show you some best practice ideas on how to overcome your negative procrastination.

## FOUR KEYS TO DEALING WITH PROCRASTINATION

Let's dive right in with some simple things you can do. These are not the only keys, of course; yet these are suggestions I've found that work for most people.

1. **Rise early**. Many people take that very last five or ten extra minutes of sleep rather than rising just a few minutes early to get up and get your momentum going. I'm suggesting that it's better to have that momentum than to be rushing around and not really building a right pace in the morning. You can overcome procrastination by getting that momentum going.

2. **Create momentum**. By identifying and doing little things when you have open minutes—like waiting between major tasks—you can get enough things happening that you will be more motivated. That momentum keeps you from procrastinating and helps you get things done.

3. **Motivate yourself.** Make to-do lists and mark things off or put an "x" by items completed. There's nothing like the satisfaction you get with accomplishment.

4. **Practice *Production Before Perfection* (PBP).** This can be the most important of all my time management concepts. It applies to most people, and that probably includes you. How many tasks are you procrastinating on right now because you want them to be too perfect? It's often best to jump in and make things happen first, and then you can perfect as you go.

Let me give you an example: Are taxes something that need to be perfect, or if not perfect, pretty close? Yes. Then does that mean you have to wait to get started on them until you get every W-2 or investment document together? No, you can start working on your taxes each month of the year, by keeping track of your taxable expenses and being organized about keeping receipts.

Now, there are a few exceptions. If you're building a Bell helicopter (I say Bell because they're one of our clients and I have discussed this with them), you have to get that pretty perfect, right? You don't want to send someone into the air unless it's pretty perfect. Or if you're a scientist, or maybe a doctor performing surgery, you want everything to be as perfect as it can be. For most people, though, whatever they're doing doesn't have to be perfect—maybe an 8 or a 9 or a 9.5. Get going, and then make it better as you go!

## ORGANIZATION

Organization is a huge time-saving tool! Let me give you six powerful tips for getting better organized:

1. **Make lists.** Yes, I know, I've said it before, and I'll say it again. And let me remind you to make sure you've using your phone. Making

lists is a key to organization, and putting your lists on your phone is crucial to making your lists work for you. Be sure your phone is organized so you can get to your lists quickly. If you take five seconds to do that now, it can save you thirty seconds each time on the back end. If you get sloppy in organizing it, it costs you time.

2. **Double up on tasks.** This is the *Elegant Solution* I introduced earlier, which is being so clear on what you want to accomplish that you can do one thing and accomplish multiple objectives. An example would be exercising and reading at the same time.

Sometimes when I go on vacation, I go with people I enjoy and who motivate me. I go with my wife and kids so I can spend time with them. I take educational activities we can use to learn together. We do fun activities. We do things that will bring us together more as a family. We talk about our future goals together. We take pictures. We recently went to Jamaica for Christmas, and we accomplished six, eight, or ten things in one vacation because we were extremely organized. I brought materials to hand out. I brought things on my computer. I even brought things to give away on our vacation. We do everything we can to maximize our vacations, experiences, meetings, events, and so on, because we're organized.

3. **Listen while you work.** No, I didn't say whistle while you work. I'm talking about listening while you work! Listen to audio books, even when you're shaving or maybe taking a bath. Take snippets from authorities who are on the web or maybe even listen to the audio version of the *RESULTS Faster!* course. (See our offer on the online SUCCESS Academy course that takes this book to another whole level.) Make sure you're listening all the time. Be organized so you'll be ready, because if you're not organized, you often won't do it. You'll procrastinate.

4. **Position your assets.** Store things around you so you can get to them—papers, supplies, batteries, or whatever that may be. Look in your briefcase or your backpack right now. Do you have your assets positioned so you can get to them? Are they organized to the max so you don't waste valuable time?

**5. Use the 3D Outline™.** The 3D Outline™ is a very powerful tool I developed almost two decades ago for organizing your presentations. What makes it so powerful is that it helps you identify three basic things—the what, the why, and the how of your presentations—right up front. When you're organizing your agenda or your outlines, don't just work with the what; make sure you organize the why (your objectives for each what) and the how (different presentation methods/options) as well, and you will be able to present so much more efficiently. When you look at the why of a segment, for example, you may not be able to justify all the time you would need for that segment, so you might trim that down. You could end up saving time on the whole presentation or the whole meeting just by looking at that one element.

**6. Organize your reading**. Keep reading materials everywhere. I keep them in my car, I keep them on my desk, I keep them in my bathrooms, and I keep them in my kitchen. I have my reading materials everywhere, nicely organized, so I can take minutes to read and continue to improve when I can, and I save minutes by not having to chasing those materials down.

## DELEGATION

Many people miss this one, even though it's so important. As we go through these, you may think, *Well, that doesn't apply to me,* and yet I'm going to show you how it does apply to you. Here are my keys to delegation:

1. **Cross-delegate.** Trade projects with your associate, friend, or spouse. My wife and I trade projects often. She doesn't want to deal with taxes or insurance. I don't want to deal with the grocery store. If I want anything, I ask her, and boom! The next day I get it. When the tax returns are ready (and we file a ton of them!), they are all organized and set up so that she just has to sign her name.

2. **Transfer ownership.** So many times when we're delegating we don't transfer the ownership of the responsibility of progress.

If you really want to be exceptional at saving time, delegate to someone and then have them update you on the progress. Seeing that they really own it and are making progress saves you from having to hound them to make sure it's getting done.

3. **Contract outside services.** This could be consultants, or it could be someone putting up your Christmas tree. It could be anything you don't have the time or the skills to do, or something you don't want to do because you can invest your time doing something more productive.

4. **Train for the future.** When you train efficiently, the person you're training may be able to do the task after just one training session. In fact, sometimes you can even train the person to do the task automatically, and you won't have to delegate it to them each time; it just shows up proactively on their plate.

5. **Use readers.** This is a little different than the readers I talked about in the Prioritization segment. I'm talking about having others read and prep for you. People ask me to look at tons of material, and I have people on my team as well as outside resources all around the world that I send material to for them to read, break it down for me, highlight it, and put it into concise documents, which I call *Smart Reports*. And guess what? Because I do this, I get to learn more than I would if I tried to do it all by myself.

Now let me give you three bonus suggestions to help you maximize your time.

1. **Schedule breaks to stay on track during the day.** Chances are you can't spend eight straight hours buried in your to-do list, so schedule a couple of breaks during the day to return calls, answer e-mail, or walk to another office to follow up on an important conversation. Just be sure not to get derailed for long.

2. **Avoid people and distractions that waste your time and energy.** Detox your life by avoiding people or distractions that aren't good for you or waste your time. This includes listening to incessant complainers or gossipers, and frittering away time

online or on your phone playing yet another game.

3. **Focus on creating *Elegant Solutions* to maximize your time.**
Remember, you create an *Elegant Solution* when you are so clear
on your objectives that you can accomplish more than one thing
at a time by combining them. Here are a few examples:

- Take a colleague or client golfing or to another sporting
event that allows you to socialize. You can solidify relationships and discuss business opportunities at the same time.

- Invite someone you're mentoring (or perhaps a new team
member) to participate in a meeting that would add value to
them and teach them simultaneously.

- Take your kids on a business trip with you to help them learn
and spend time together while you're working.

- Plan a business lunch or happy hour at a popular networking
spot to connect with others at the same time.

- Select places to vacation where your family can learn a new
culture or experience something new while also spending
quality time together. Talk about your goals on the trip.

- Host an event that both brings value to your clients and connects them with others who can bring value to them.

- Work out with a business colleague or client.

Now let's move on to *Presentation Mastery*™ and see how it can
escalate your results!

# Presentation Mastery™

Have you ever considered that life truly is a series of presentations?
In every encounter you have—whether it's with a colleague, a friend,
a customer, or your spouse—you're presenting yourself. And you're
representing yourself and/or your business. The way you present your
thoughts and ideas to people really does make a difference, whether
it's to someone waiting in line at a grocery store or to someone you

just met. Your presentation can have a profound impact and shape someone's life, or it can be the key to whether someone takes action on your behalf.

As I mentioned earlier, I wrote a book a few years ago called *Life Is a Series of Presentations*, which was published by Simon and Schuster, and again I was fortunate to get an outstanding endorsement out of the blue from Daymond John with *Shark Tank* when he mentioned this book as one of the six top all-time books anyone in business should read. It's one of my favorite best-sellers that I've ever authored, and I am going to bring that content to life for you in this section.

There are three things we want to accomplish in this section:

1. We're going to raise your awareness that life truly is a series of presentations.

2. We're going to help you understand that presentation/communication is more than a skillset. It's really a strategic asset for both an individual and an organization. How well you present matters!

3. We're going to share some techniques for really increasing your business growth, and we'll have some fun while we're at it.

Presentation/communication, both personally and professionally, is more than a skillset. It's a strategic asset. Good presentation skills will allow you to:

- Build your confidence and your ability to influence your audience.

- Leverage opportunities to increase leads, close more deals, and build profits.

- Facilitate execution and inspire action.

- Maximize meetings for effectiveness and efficiency.

PRESENTATION/ COMMUNICATION, BOTH PERSONALLY AND PROFESSIONALLY, IS MORE THAN A SKILLSET. IT'S A STRATEGIC ASSET.

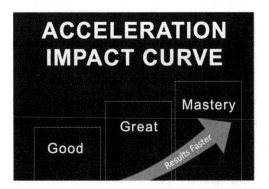

The goal, then, is to work toward mastery on the presentation impact curve, and here's how that works: Some people stay at the good level, some people move to great, and some people live in the mastery level where they see the greatest results. I like helping people—you—move into mastery.

How many presentations do you give each week, on average? Think about that question for a minute. Is it five? Ten? Fifteen? I'm going to bet it's hundreds, and here's why: We're presenting by e-mail all the time. We're presenting by phone all the time. We're presenting delayed presentations in voicemail all the time. We're presenting to our kids, to our spouse, to our neighbors. As a matter of fact, when we get up in the morning we present to ourselves. Right? When we're brushing our teeth, don't we talk to ourselves and say things like, *It's going to be a wonderful day*, or *Man, I dread this day*? Life truly is a series of presentations.

How effective are you in making presentations? Whether you think you are a one or a ten, let me challenge you to think about these three things: *How well do you prepare? How well do you deliver? And how well do you follow up?* We want to push that number up as I give you my best presentation principles in this chapter.

To get started, I want you to think more in depth about your presentation universe. What types of presentations are you involved in? Do you present at staff meetings? On video? In speeches? Do you present to your colleagues? In trade shows? To your wife? To your kids? At church? To your neighbors? Do you present in conference calls? In trainings? On the web? Think about all the presentations you make in your universe, and get that picture in your head so you can apply each of the principles I'm about to give you.

Opportunities are missed every day in business. How about boring meetings? How many meetings do you lead that are boring? How about ineffective sales presentations? Maybe the people who work for you—or maybe you—give botched presentations and speeches that fail to connect. Opportunities are missed every day because people don't do what I am about to share. I am leading up to the eight critical principles from *Life Is a Series of Presentations*; however, before we get there let me round this out a little bit more.

There are ten types of presentations that happen every day inside an organization: sales presentations, meetings, trainings, facilitating, branding (including on the web), speeches, seminars, interactions with the media, one-on-one, and e-presentations! We're going to be touching on all ten of those.

## TWELVE QUESTIONS

I have twelve questions for you, and we're going to have some fun with this, so get ready.

1. **Approximately how many words per minute does the average person speak?**

    A. 500

    B. 100

    C. 200

    D. 400

    *The answer is…C, 200! We speak at about 200 words a minute.*

2. **Approximately how many words per minute can the average person effectively hear and process?**

    A. 500

    B. 600

    C. 700

    D. 800

    *The answer is D, 800! So what's the big takeaway here? We process about four times as fast as we speak. Have you ever seen people zoning out when you're talking to them? It's because they can outthink the pace in which you're talking. This is important. If you really want to master this subject, you have to understand that people really do get distracted because they can outthink you.*

3. **Which of the following aspects of communication is most perceived by an audience?**

 A. The spoken word

 B. Body language

 C. Tone of voice

 D. Room color and scheme

 *The answer is B, body language, followed closely behind with C, tone of voice. What does that mean to you? That means you have to use your body, and you have to think about that the entire time you're presenting. Sometimes we don't even catch what we're doing, and we should. For example, when we're talking to one of our kids, we might need to step back and be more open with our body language instead of being in their face. Body language is so powerful.*

4. **What is the length of the average adult attention span?**

 A. 15 to 20 minutes

 B. 27 to 31 minutes

 C. 5 to 7 minutes

 D. 12 to 15 minutes

 *Best answer: C, 5 to 7 minutes, or even less! It keeps going down every year! Think about attention spans today. We really live in an ADD (attention deficit disorder) culture, so you have to make things quick for people.*

5. **The method used to get consistent feedback from the audience during a presentation is called:**

 A. Targeted Questioning

 B. Verbal Surveying

 C. Testing the waters

 D. Business entertainment

*The best answer is B, Verbal Surveying. When you get about one-third into your presentation, survey the audience and ask, "Is there something I need to change? Do I need to go into a little bit more detail? Do I need to go a little faster? How's the pace?" Instead of waiting until the end to get feedback, Verbally Survey the audience and make changes based on their feedback while you're presenting.*

**6. What comes first in determining the objectives of a presentation?**

A. Defining the audience

B. Knowing the action the audience should take

C. Knowing how many people will be in the audience

D. Both A and B.

*You guessed it! Both A and B—defining the audience and knowing the action you want your audience to take.*

**7. What's the major cause of nervousness? Almost everybody gets nervous at some time.**

A. Claustrophobia

B. Low self-esteem

C. Fear of the unknown

D. Paranoia

*The best answer is C, fear of the unknown. When we take every unknown to the known, then our confidence level goes up. When I walk onto a stage before I give a presentation, I've already turned my unknowns into knowns. My team has already sent me pictures of the stage, my views from the stage, and the audience's views, so I don't have to worry about setup. And before the presentation, I look for every possible way I can pretest the mic so I feel comfortable with the technical aspects. I even know things like when I am going to walk onto the stage to meet the person who is introducing me and when and where we're going to shake hands. Turning every unknown into a known allows you to be less nervous and more impactful!*

**8. What's one of the best ways to build rapport with an audience?**

A. Start early

B. Skip lunch

C. Talk about commonalities

D. Spell their names right

*It's C, talk about commonalities. People really connect with you when you talk about the things you have in common.*

9. **In a presentation environment, one of the best ways to reduce nervousness is**

A. Take a valium

B. Preparation

C. Avoidance

D. Procrastination

*It's B, preparation! The more prepared you are, the more you've taken the unknowns to the known.*

10. **Which one of the following is an effective way to establish credibility and gain 100 percent audience buy in?**

A. Trust transference

B. Be yourself

C. Tell the truth

D. All of the above

*You got it! It's D, all of the above. It's so important to transfer the trust of others. And it's also important to be real, to be yourself, and obviously to tell the truth!*

11. **During your presentation, one of the best ways to reduce nervousness is:**

A. Read from your notes. (I read from my notes for the first time in decades just a few months ago, when I gave a tribute at my dad's funeral. I got up and said at the beginning, "Normally I wouldn't do this; however, I've actually written out my speech so I can read it, because I think I might cry. I know you guys don't mind, right? My dad was so incredible that I wanted to give this tribute to him." Then I showed forty slides that highlighted the best parts of his life. I really had to read some of the messages because of my emotions; however, I started out by saying, "How many of you think funerals are boring?" Everyone just looked at me for a minute, so I said, "No, come on. Raise your hand if you think funerals are boring." Then they all started raising their hands, and I said, "Well, this one is not going to be boring, because my dad wasn't boring. He was inspiring, and I want to give a tribute to his life." So I got audience involvement, and I used many of the concepts we're talking about here in this chapter. The next day the e-mails started coming in: "Best funeral ever!" I may have had to read the notes; however, I did all the other things to make it impactful.)

B. Get the audience involved

C. Don't look at the audience

D. Look over the heads of the audience

*The best answer is B, get them involved! What did I do at my dad's funeral? I had people raise their hands. What am I doing with you now? I'm asking you questions and getting you involved with this little quiz before we get into the heavier content.*

**12. Which of the following best summarizes our task of meeting audiences' expectations?**

A. Learning and using audience members' names

B. Creating winning opportunities

C. Being flexible

D. Giving value—doing more than is expected

*Look at those choices for a moment. The best answer is D, giving value and doing more than expected. That is my mantra. Are you looking at every presentation and doing everything you can to give value and do more than is expected?*

There you have it—twelve compelling questions, twelve best answers, and twelve things that you should really absorb.

## EIGHT POWERFUL PRACTICES

Now I want to move into the core content of this section, which is also the core content of *Life Is a Series of Presentations*—eight powerful practices! You see, I've been doing research on this subject for over two decades. First I narrowed it down to sixty strategic practices, which was too much. Then I narrowed it down again to the eight most powerful. There is one word that defines each of them, so I came up with the mnemonic I PRESENT.

**I**—Involve the audience! One of the best ways to do this is ask questions or have people write things down. When they write things down, they get engaged. And here's another win: Their eyes go down, and you get a breathing space. In almost every speech I give, whether it's to 200 people or 20,000 people, I start with a question. Even at my dad's funeral, I started with a question. Even when I get on the phone, I start with a question. Ask questions and get people involved. So many times we talk too much, and we don't ask for involvement enough.

**P**—Prepare your audience. Many times in today's world we invite people to a meeting or another type of presentation, and we fail to list the rich benefits they'll get when they attend. I also encourage you to touch people before you talk. That means going out and shaking hands with the members of your audience, whether it's ten people or 200 or 2,000. Also, incorporate a strong host introduction, and then open with a solid payoff. The first thing you say really does matter. People start absorbing right away.

**R**—Research and build a powerful presentation arsenal. Start with a mental arsenal of things you keep in your mind. For example, I was at church years ago and I watched a guy who was substituting for our pastor put flip charts on the front of the stage. Now, there were about 1,000 people in the congregation that day, and I was thinking, *What is this dude doing? Flip charts with 1,000 people? He hasn't read my books! You don't use flip charts with 1,000 people!* And then he fooled me. He had four flip charts and one big, fat marker. During his presentation, he spelled out one very impactful four-letter word by putting one letter on each flip chart that represented each of his four points. He had me. I thought, Wow! I guess you can use flip charts with 1,000 people.

So I put that in my mental arsenal, and since that time I've used flip charts differently.

Look around and build your arsenal with ideas you can save and use for the future. That includes things you can use in an electronic arsenal—with things you have in your phone, for example—and it includes hard copy and material props, like things you can give away.

**E**—Explain the why! This is so powerful, and yet people miss it all the time! Make sure to give the why by using words like "because" and "so that." It's so important to do that in every presentation—even in an e-mail! I might say, for example, "One of the things I encourage you to do is build an outstanding arsenal so that you're more content rich when you need to give a presentation."

I've been in Sydney, Australia several times in the last few years, and I'm very fascinated with the Sydney Opera House. The architecture is very intriguing, which includes quite a few angled panels. On one of the panels there is a sign that says, "In the interest of safety do not climb on angled panels." Notice they gave the why, "in the interest of safety," before they asked for the action. Giving the people the why helps them take ownership.

**S**—State management. If you're giving a presentation to a group of ten or more, you will probably have all these states in your audience:

1. The vacationer, who's really not a troublemaker; they're just vacationing.
2. The prisoner, who has their arms crossed and really doesn't want to be there.
3. The graduates—the people who know it all.
4. The students, who are really there to learn and absorb.

A master presenter is continually moving people to the student mentality so they want to hear what they have to say.

**E**—Eliminating the unknowns. As we talked about in the quiz above, turning every unknown into the known adds confidence. I was walking through my home about twelve years ago when my oldest daughter was about ten years old, and I saw her doing something that fascinated me. She had a presentation to give the next day at school, and she was preparing for it. I was blown away by what I saw, and I thought, *Man, I have to take a picture of this and use it in my work.* She was rehearsing in front of her dolls! She had heard dad talk about rehearsing and preparing, and there she was, presenting in front of her dolls.

**N**—kNow your audience! Create a mental profile of your audience members, which could include age, background, education, and occupation. Survey your audience members ahead of your presentation through e-mail, if possible, and talk to them one on one before you start your presentation. It's important to understand your audience so you can target your objectives to meet their particular needs.

**T**—Tailor your presentation! I developed a concept called *Planned Spontaneity,* which is being so prepared in advance that you can be flexible and ready to adjust your presentation to fit whatever issues may come up from your audience. *Planned Spontaneity* is a quality that separates the master presenters from those who are merely good.

So there you have the eight I PRESENT concepts from my best-selling book, *Life is a Series of Presentations.* I encourage you to study these eight concepts and use them to help you take your presentations to the highest level—*Presentation Mastery*™.

By learning to manage your time intentionally and by achieving *Presentation Mastery*™, you'll move that needle forward toward executing well and achieving your vision. Finally, there's one more area to help you execute that will propel your vision forward even more quickly in this fast-paced world, and that's *Strategic Selling*.

# STRATEGIC SELLING

Life is not only a series of presentations; it's also a series of persuasions! So this concept of *Strategic Selling* is going to be valuable to you, no matter who you are. **We are all in some type of sales position, whether we're physically selling products or services or attempting to influence others in any capacity, either personally or professionally.** Any time you need to influence or persuade someone, you are "selling" them on your idea or position. For example, you need to "sell" your kids on going to bed at a particular hour or eating a particular food. You need to "sell" your spouse on buying the car or TV or appliance you want. You need to "sell" your co-workers on helping you with a project, and you need to "sell" your boss on the results you produced. You even need to "sell" yourself on doing some of the things you learned in this book! Selling is simply persuading someone to take a specific action. You do this all the time, and it's a key skill for getting anything done in this world, or executing. Being more strategic about the process and dissecting the opportunities to understand all the people you influence and all the desired outcomes can dramatically increase the likelihood of getting the results you want.

> LIFE IS NOT ONLY A SERIES OF PRESENTATIONS; IT'S ALSO A SERIES OF PERSUASIONS!

We're going to go through this in four segments. The first segment is about awareness. Then in the second segment I'll touch on a few skills. In the third segment, I'll give you a few powerful processes. And then in the fourth segment I'll give you many useful tools. All four areas can help you be more strategic and sell your products, services, or ideas to get people to take action, ensuring you get execution.

## Part One: Awareness

There are seven keys to share in this area of awareness:

1. **Know the type of opportunity you have in front of you.** This distinction is so valuable. Think through it. Is it a one-time opportunity? Is it a medium or large opportunity? Is it transactional? Is it a long-term strategic opportunity? Will it introduce you to other opportunities?

If you're presenting to your kids, you don't want to mess up the "bank account" you have with them by pushing them to do something. You want to be strategic because you want to deposit into that long-term relationship. I have incredible daughters; and as I've maneuvered through raising them, I didn't push things too hard when I when I wanted to sell them on something because I looked at the long-term relationship.

If I am selling to someone and they say, "I want to start with a one-day relationship with you," I think about the potential. If they're a big organization and they fit my ADOME profile, I think, *Is there potential for a long-term relationship here? Are there multiple impacts? What's the size of the opportunity? How about any future opportunities that might follow?*

2. **Know your stakeholders.** Being fully aware of what everyone wants and what they can give is often not on the radar screen of an organizational strategy session, and yet it should be.

When we bring people in to my *Strategic Acceleration* studio, we pop up on the screen a template that we invented, a Stakeholder's Matrix. We ask them to list in the first column all of the stakeholders involved—such as the shareholders, the board, the CEO, the executive leaders, the partners, the associates, and the employees. When you're really being strategic, you think about how you will impact every person who is a stakeholder. In a family situation, remember the grandparents. How will they see the opportunity? Look at it from the parents' point of view. From the kids' point of view. From the point of view of other families. It's so important that everyone involved is aware of the whole picture.

3. **Look at the presentation phases.** Is it a one-time presentation to get the action you want, or will it take two or three steps? For example, you may introduce something to your spouse and/or your kids, and then a week later you introduce some more things to them, and finally the third time you get them to say "yes." This applies both in business and on the personal side. Recognize where you are in the phases.

4. **Gather your intelligence strategically.** Information is powerful. The more you know, the more power you put into your own hands. How well do you research and gather intelligence?

As I said earlier, *Smart Reports* are a big part of my life, and I encourage them with the executives I work with. Having their teams gather intelligence for them so they really know who they're talking to when they're presenting or selling helps them be their best. Social media, especially LinkedIn, is a fantastic way to get information. And use your network of connections; call someone or send them an e-mail to get your intelligence. Be strategic about everything! Figure out what you really want. Clarity creates pulling power! I've said it before, and I'll say it again: Clarity has major influence on you and those around you.

5. **Know your competition.** As part of the intelligence gathering process, in most cases you will dramatically increase your odds of closing a deal if you know and understand your competition. Be able to articulate and differentiate what makes your value proposition unique to all the others out there.

6. **Remember that people buy, not companies.** Your relationships are with people. So many times we in the business world get confused. We try to sell to the benefits of the company. It's much more effective to know the people and then sell to the benefits of the people.

7. **Figure out what you really want.** Clarity creates pulling power. I know, I've said that several times, and now I'm saying it again. It has a major influence on you and those around you. For example, do you want a long-term relationship? If you're clear on that, you will be stronger. Remember, people buy, not companies.

## Part Two: Sharpening and Polishing Your Skills

I'm going to give you ten important skills you need to work on and sharpen. Some of these may overlap with what we discussed in the I PRESENT model, and yet they're important enough to consider again.

> REMEMBER THAT PEOPLE BUY, NOT COMPANIES.

1. **Use different communication approaches.** Know what works for your receiver. So many times we get stuck in *our* preferences. Maybe we prefer e-mail, although the recipient prefers text. Do they want to communicate verbally, through the web, or in person? Again, think about your kids. How do kids want to communicate today? They want text. My mom is older, so sometimes when I'm communicating with my mom I write things. Think about who you're communicating with and how they want to receive your message. Then get good at it.

2. **Strategically listen to needs!** Improve your ability to listen.

Let me tell you a story. I spent a year working with the CEO of a big consulting firm that was thinking about hiring me. Now, this was a multi-million-dollar opportunity! After a year we finally got the chairman to fly in and sit down with me. Everything was set, locked, and loaded. All I had to do was meet the guy, and I just knew that he would be ready to go forward. So we met for a couple of hours, and he started asking me question after question after question—and I answered question after question after question. Then they left, and I was thinking, *Man, we had an outstanding meeting.* I called the CEO and asked, "What did the chairman think?" You can imagine my shock when he said, "We can't hire you." "What do you mean, you can't hire me?" I asked. "We spent a year on this." And he said, "You didn't listen! You fell into the trap that we wanted to avoid." Wow! I really had to talk to myself and ask, *What's going on here?* He was exactly right. I wasn't listening. This is what I needed to learn: Don't just be interesting; be interested. Strategic listening does pay.

3. **Help others win!** So many times people are all about themselves,

and they don't look for ways to reinforce other people winning. When you're in a meeting, you have many opportunities to influence someone. For example, when someone shares a good idea, validate it! Use words like, "Tell me more," and let them win! When they win, they feel good, their emotions go up, and you get more connected, right? And when you get more connected, they get more behind your idea.

4. **Show people the clear picture!** Clarity of your vision is so important, and you need to be able to communicate that to everyone involved. Communicate what you really want up front. Do you want them to include a certain step? Do you want a particular deadline? That's part of the clear picture they need to see. Communicate it well!

5. **Present to people the way they want to receive information.** Engaged participants win, and if they win, you win. Don't get stuck in your style or your preferences. Do it their way.

6. **Give people the why.** I talked about this earlier in the I PRESENT model. The why is so valuable. When you provide the reasoning behind what you are asking of others, people will take action much more quickly.

7. **Be early and be *Presentation Ready*.** Have all necessary tools and information organized and ready to go, and be ready to share them and take notes, even at a moment's notice.

8. **Be flexible and communicate in a style that matches theirs.** We're talking about personality style here. Dr. Robert Rohm and I wrote a book together some years back called *Presenting with Style*. It's a powerful book, using the DISC Model of Human Behavior. Dr. Rohm has taught me so much as he's talked about how he has raised his kids according to their personality styles and about understanding the distinctions of a person's style and presenting accordingly.

If a person has a style of a driver (D), for example, what do they want? They want to receive information fast and without too many details. If a person is more of an influencer (I), their style is happy-go-lucky, and they're really into socialization. You want to make sure you communicate with them with some humor and fun. If they're more stable and steady (S) and into process, then you want to strategically answer and communicate in steps. And if they're very cautious (C), communicate to them with a number of details.

9. **Show people how to help you.** Show the process, steps, and actions you'd like to include and how they win, and you'll have a winning formula.

10. **Practice *Planned Spontaneity*.** As we discussed in the I PRESENT model, *Planned Spontaneity* is simply being so prepared going into your presentation that you can spontaneously react to your attendees in a way that matters most to them.

## Part Three: Process

When you add the processes to your skills, it really pushes you up a level. I want to give you three big distinctions about process.

1. **Really qualify your prospect.** I shared with you the process we go through to qualify our prospects according to the ADOME profile. It's important to qualify your prospect or opportunity before you invest tons of energy into making the connection. Many times we put too much energy into something that we shouldn't, and we get burned.

2. **Define the situation, needs, value, outcomes, deliverables, and terms.** Having a 360-degree view of the landscape is essential to putting together a winning deal for everyone.

Situation: a detailed overview/summary

Needs: what the client wants or wants to avoid

Value: what we can uniquely provide and how it will help them

Outcomes: the real deal of what they want

Deliverables: exactly what the prospect will receive from our offering to help them get the outcome they want

Terms: the business agreement

Use this as a process to really prepare well every time you have a major opportunity to sell.

3. **Leverage the 3D Outline™ process.** We've talked about it before; however, it's such a powerful tool that it warrants going over it again. This is a process for getting your objectives clear and then building an outline to make sure your objectives are met. Make sure you're clear on the objectives first, and then use the outline to support reaching your objectives.

Once you have your objectives down, look at *what* you're going to say, *why* you're going to say it, and *how* you're going to deliver it. All three matter, and yet most people just look at the what. I'm encouraging you as part of the process to look at the why for each what, and then look at the how. You can go to strategicacceleration.com/resources (click on Exercise 14) to download a 3D™ Outline template.

## Part Four: Tools

This last segment is about leveraging a robust arsenal of tools, and I'll give you four specific tools you can use.

1. **Leverage testimonials.** We all know that social proof really does matter. People do what other people do, and yet most people don't build a testimonial arsenal to take advantage of that. It can be as simple as keeping quotes and one-liners on your phone, or you can keep letters or referrals in your computer, or you can take pictures of cards or nice notes you've received from your happy customers. Make sure you really build and leverage an exemplary testimonial arsenal.

2. **Share case studies.** Well-chosen case studies showcase similar situations to your prospects in which you've provided a fantastic solution. I've developed a system I'd like to share with you. If you've done something for somebody and it works, define what the problem was, what you did to provide the solution, and what the outcomes or results

PEOPLE DO WHAT OTHER PEOPLE DO, AND YET MOST PEOPLE DON'T BUILD A TESTIMONIAL ARSENAL TO TAKE ADVANTAGE OF THAT.

were. It's that simple! Keep it simple so people will understand it!

3. **Prepare an objections matrix.** Whether you're selling to your kid, your spouse, a friend, a CEO, or anyone else, make sure you've taken the time in advance to determine what their objections or potential push back might be, and be prepared with the best ways to answer them.

---

Let's do a little quiz. What would your response be to the following objections?

- We have a limited budget. How can your product or service provide ROI/ROE for us?

- We can't get people together to make a decision.

- What if I want different options than you're illustrating?

While you're considering your responses, think about the lead person that should take on the objection if it's a group presentation.

---

4. **Think through the "what ifs."** Have you ever been in a situation where one of the three decision makers didn't show up for your sales presentation? You need to think about what you would do (the "what if") if that happened. Or what would you do if you expected three or four people and seven showed up? Do you have extra handouts? Think about the five or ten most feasible "what ifs" that could happen and make sure you're ready and covered for those to give you the best influence for getting the results you want.

Well, now you're equipped with all three components of my powerful *Strategic Acceleration* formula: Clarity, Focus, and Execution. Study these concepts, master them, and put them to work in your business and personal life, and you'll see RESULTS faster than you've ever seen!

In the next chapter I'll share with you some powerful ideas that will multiply and enhance your results even more!

# V.I.P.s

- Where and how you invest your time and energy will determine your results! Period!

- You can maximize your time by using four tools: prioritization, avoiding procrastination, organization, and delegation.

- Life truly is a series of presentations.

- Presentation/communication is more than a skillset. It's a strategic asset.

- Being strategic versus just being skillful can greatly impact the results you get.

- Life is not only a series of presentations; it's also a series of persuasions!

## CHAPTER 5:

# FORCE MULTIPLIERS

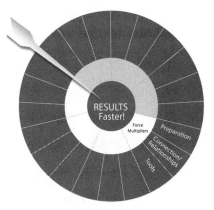

Now that you have the *Strategic Acceleration* formula down—Clarity, Focus and Execution—wouldn't it be great if you could multiply those efforts? Well, you can. I'm going to show you specific ideas in this chapter on how you can use what I call "force multipliers" that will help you get even better results, even faster.

Exactly what is a "force multiplier"? **It's a factor that dramatically increases (multiplies) the effectiveness of something you're doing.** In the military, it's a term that applies to a capability that significantly increases the combat potential of a military force and thus enhances the probability of a successful mission. One example would be night goggles. If a combat force goes into a particular area at night, night goggles would significantly enhance their chances of a successful mission. A force multiplier for a taekwondo martial artist may be the employment of pressure points in combat.

I use pre- and post-workout force multipliers every time I work out. For example, my trainers are very specific about having me eat certain proteins and complex carbohydrates exactly forty-five minutes before I train, because they multiply the efforts toward what I want to accomplish by keeping my energy up as I work out.

**A force multiplier, then, refers to any factor that dramatically increases your results in whatever you're doing.** It's really about leverage. Wouldn't you like to multiply every effort you make? Remember, if you change your thinking, you'll change your results. I want to take you to a new place in your thinking, a place where few people go, so you can multiply your results.

I'm going to share with you in this chapter three primary force-multiplier components: preparation, connections, and tool chest. And let me tell you, I'm passionate about all three.

I believe most people don't prepare as well as they could. Do you fall into that category? I'm talking about preparing to the extreme—I call it *Planned Spontaneity*—even to the point that you make sure you get the right amount of rest, you put yourself in the right mental state, and you do everything you possibly can to be super ready.

Chances are there are multiple areas in your personal and professional life where you can get better results by preparing more effectively. I've found that most people prepare for major events and opportunities, and yet few people prepare strategically and as wide as they should. Remember what I said at the beginning of this book about being *Intentionally Strategic* in everything you do? I'm going to share with you how to be *Intentionally Strategic* in your preparation.

Then we'll talk about your connections, which are one of the most significant force multipliers you can have. The first key to leveraging relationships is to **build them**. Once you have them, it's about nurturing them—knowing what's important to them, being a giver in the relationship, and being willing to introduce them to each other for mutual benefit.

You can have a long list of connections, and yet if you don't nourish them, what do you think will happen when you need to call in a favor? Not much! Be a person of value in all your relationships so there is never a question of whether they will respond if you call. Today I can make phone calls or send e-mails all around the world, and people respond instantly. Why? Because I nourish people. I want to give you some of my best practices on how to nourish the people in your life. You can use your relationships to help you multiply your efforts, gain intelligence, and get things done.

Finally, we'll talk about your tool chest, which is another of my favorite subjects. We may all have a great electronic tool chest—in our phones, for instance, where we've downloaded certain software or applications—and yet there's so much more. There are undoubtedly tools specific to your particular situation or business that can provide leverage. For example, in the area of marketing you may have tools like videos, promotional pieces, and smart giveaways. Do you have the right tools? And do you keep tools in all the different places you operate so you can easily get to them when you connect with people? Everywhere I go I'm loaded with tools (items of value I can easily share), because I know the power of their leverage.

The best tools—whether they are the hottest technological devices out there, innovative marketing pieces, or great tools that help you plan and prepare—will help give you the leverage you need to get the extraordinary results you want. In the turbulent climate of change today, you must seize advantages where you can.

I'm excited to share with you these force-multiplying concepts that I've shared with many people all around the world. Let's get started.

# PREPARATION

Let me start by asking, how well do you prepare? Think for a minute and rate yourself on a scale of 1 to 10. Do you do a great job in preparing, which puts you at about an 8 or a 9? Maybe you're somewhere in the middle—perhaps a 4 or 5—and you know you need to do better. Or perhaps you're way down on the chart and you're saying, "That's definitely something I need to work on." Wherever you are on that spectrum, we're going to help you push that needle further up the scale.

I'm going to start with four personal examples, and then we'll roll into six specific things I do that can help you be your very best.

Here's my first example: I'm fortunate to have different trainers, and I often rotate them. Then each night before my training, I go to bed early, about 7:30 or 8:00. Now I don't always go to sleep right away; I may just rest for about an hour and a half or so, and then I'm asleep by 9:00. Why? Because I get up early to work with my trainers, and I want to be prepared and rested so I can get the maximum benefit from my workout.

Right before I go to bed I get a little hungry, like most people. Since casein protein helps my metabolism and sets me up to have a really great workout the next morning, I usually have a casein shake. Then, as I mentioned earlier, I load myself up with carbs and proteins the next morning, forty-five minutes before my trainer arrives. I get myself into the right mindset, and when I go out into my gym, I'm ready to go. How about you? Are you taking your health and the preparation for your body to the highest level?

Here's the next example: Before I work with new clients, I research and study them carefully. I learn about their histories, their personalities, and their priorities. My team finds out all they can about them, their companies, and their competitors through reports from Dunn & Bradstreet. I have my team study everything they can, including trends in their industry, and provide *Smart Reports* for me. I study past notes from previous meetings and conversations so I'm really prepared when I start working with them. It's a level of preparation most don't bother with. It makes a difference in the results I can deliver for them. When I start my conversations with them, they are often very impressed because of the level of detail I know about their particular industry. I don't necessarily try to be an expert in every industry. I'm an expert at helping people get results, and one of the pieces to that puzzle is extreme preparation.

Now think about your level of preparation for working with your customers, clients, boss, team, board, and so on. Are you taking it to the highest level by researching who they are, their priorities, their biases, and other information on them so you'll be ready to work with or for them?

My third example involves preparing my two daughters for life. You may remember that my wife and I made the decision sixteen years ago to shrink my company and build a special private studio on my estate so I could work here and we could pour extra energy into our kids. For twenty years we stepped back on other things so we could prepare them for life. We envisioned what they would become. Our real desire over all those years was that they would be highly successful when they launched out of the nest, so we recognized that the real payoff would be revealed two decades later. At the time of this writing, our daughters are nineteen and twenty-two, and we couldn't be more pleased with the bright, happy, successful, and giving young ladies they are today! We put in a great deal of preparation, and it was well worth the effort.

Think about how you're preparing your kids for life, no matter how old they are. Are you preparing them to launch out successfully? Or perhaps you're at a stage in your life where you have grandkids, and you can help them prepare for life. **Preparation is not just for the short term; it's also for the long term.**

Here's my last example: Before I am the keynote at an event, I often have my team go on ahead to look over and set up the venue. They send me pictures so can I see where I'm going to stand, and so I can see the audience view from different angles in the room or stadium. When I see the pictures, it helps me start preparing in my mind so I can be my best when I get there. They check out the microphone system and set everything out. In the meantime, I review my notes over and over so I can enjoy what I've termed *Planned Spontaneity*. Because I'm prepared and planned on the front end, I can be spontaneous and genuine in the moment, and that makes a huge difference to the audience. Having everything prepared in such detail ahead of time allows me to be so connected when I arrive that I can create a great experience with the people I'm talking to.

I want to know my audience. In fact, I often go out and shake hands with audience members before the event starts, even if there are 10,000 people there, because I want to be connected to them. That's part of preparing my state of mind.

To what extent do you prepare before a presentation, whether it's to one person or 1,000? Are you using preparation as a competitive advantage and a force multiplier?

Now, I promised to give you six specifics that will help you prepare well. You may want to take notes or highlight these six, because I really want you to push the envelope here. Preparation is so important!

## SIX EASY WAYS TO MAKE YOUR PREPARATION A SECRET TO YOUR SUCCESS

1. **Mental ownership**. Mentally own preparation as a differentiator. In any situation, there is always someone who's the most prepared. Decide now that you're going to be that person, and make it part of your brand. A mindset that says, *I will always prep and be ready ahead of time* is simply a philosophy that sparks success.

> IN ANY SITUATION, THERE IS ALWAYS SOMEONE WHO'S THE MOST PREPARED. DECIDE NOW THAT YOU'RE GOING TO BE THAT PERSON, AND MAKE IT PART OF YOUR BRAND.

As I've traveled the world, working in over forty countries over a period of thirty years, I've never been a minute late. I've always been there, always on time. My mental commitment is that I'm going to be prepared and ready. How about yours?

2. **Templates**. Build tools that will help with your prep. I'm talking about tools that are specific to preparation. Our team has several things we do that are crucial to great preparation. Let's talk about a couple of them.

**Event checklist**. One thing I encourage you to do—before you go meet someone, before you go make a presentation, or before you prepare for any event—is to make an event checklist that reminds you of all the things that need to be done. When we open an event file, we look on the left side where the checklist is to see what's been sent ahead, who we're meeting with, what the objectives are, what the background is, and anything else that's pertinent to that event. It's all broken down so it's easy to see if anything has slipped through the cracks. An event checklist is a very powerful tool.

**Notes template.** Have you ever noticed that most people don't take good notes in meetings? If you use a good notes template, fill it in throughout the meeting, and send it to all the participants later, they can see all of the pertinent pieces. Much of it can be prepared in advance. At the top of our notes template, we list who is in attendance. Then we list the objectives, the agenda, the expectations, and the most important points. Then we list who is supposed to take action, along with the actions they're going to take and by what date. And finally we list any closing comments. A good notes template is right up there with the 3D Outline™ that I've mentioned before. They are both excellent tools that literally change the dynamics of your preparation.

I encourage you be innovative as you're building a great tool chest. Look for tools you can buy or make yourself, or even tools you can borrow that will help you be really prepared. You can even make a tool that will help you prepare for traveling. Build a checklist and keep it on your phone, so you'll be sure to pack all the things you need.

3. **People.** Surround yourself with people who help you prepare well. Some of these people may work for you directly, like an executive assistant or a communications director, or maybe someone who travels with you. Others may be colleagues or a family member. When my wife and I travel together on vacations and other trips, we hardly ever forget anything because we help each other double check and prepare. Make sure you have people around you who are committed to helping you prepare and be your best.

4. **Self-talk.** "What can I do to be ready?" That's a powerful question we should be asking ourselves all the time. You already know that I really believe in the power of self-talk. Many people say, "I don't really do self-talk," and you may be saying that to yourself right now. Well, guess what? That's self-talk. We all talk to ourselves. So while you're

at it, ask yourself, *What can I do to be ready—and not just ready, but super ready? Is there anything else I can remember?* I suggest you don't say, *I don't want to forget this*, because "forget" is a negative embedded command. Make it positive: *What do I need to remember to be ready?* or *What can I do to be more ready?*

5. **Homework**. Do your homework. Google and other online tools have taken prep to exponentially higher levels, both in terms of the amount of information you can consume and the speed at which you can get it. Before you go meet with someone new, researching the person on Google, looking up their history on LinkedIn, or just reading their website are a few of the many options available to you. Or you can call a contact you know is connected to that person to get more information. Access today is easier than ever before; it simply takes discipline to find it.

> WHEN YOU ARE PREPARING FOR ANY EVENT, ASK YOURSELF, *WHAT COULD POSSIBLY HAPPEN?* BRAINSTORM WITH YOUR TEAM MEMBERS ABOUT WHAT COULD HAPPEN AHEAD, AND RESOLVE ANY ROADBLOCKS IN ADVANCE.

6. **Roadblock busting**. I'm going to be referring to this key concept throughout the book, and this segment on preparation is a great place to introduce it. I call it "the what ifs." When you are preparing for any event, ask yourself, *What could possibly happen?* If you're going swimming with your child, for example, what are some of the "what ifs" that could happen? If you're going to go meet with your boss, what are the "what ifs"? When you're making a presentation or leading an important meeting with a client, what could happen? What are the potential roadblocks? If more people attend than you're expecting, have you prepared enough handouts or samples? If you have a team, brainstorm with your team members

about any "what ifs" that could happen ahead of time and resolve any roadblocks in advance.

These are my six ways to achieve impeccable preparation. Now let's move on to see how your connections and relationships can multiply your results many times over.

# Connections and Relationships

Relationships can be a powerful force multiplier.

Let me tell you a story about how this mindset was imparted to me. As I was growing up, my family owned a car-cleaning business. We paid attention to detailing—all the distinctions that made a car look beautiful. That exposure was very valuable for me, and I'm so grateful that I was able to learn through it how to serve people and give more value than they expected.

Without even realizing he was doing it, my dad modeled for me how to build relationships. He had an old-fashioned desk in his shop where he kept stacks of business cards he'd collected, held together by rubber bands. He had quite a few of them—in my young mind it seemed like thousands, even though there were probably only hundreds. I remember that when he needed advice on something or needed a favor, he would open his desk and thumb through those cards. And it never took him long to find the exact card he was looking for. Within minutes he would make a phone call and connect with the person who could help him. That may have been a person who could open a door for me as a young entrepreneur or someone who could help us solve a problem, or it may have been someone he could get information or order a part from. He had a card for virtually every need. I grew up watching him do that, and it made a huge impression on me. There was a powerful lesson there that was deeply imbedded in my mind—if you want to really be successful in life, let's face it: you pretty much have to have good connections. I was fascinated by that at a young age, and I've been modeling it ever since.

Now, let's talk about you. When you meet someone new and that person gives you a business card, what do you do with it? If you're like many people I've seen, instead of entering the person's information into whatever system you have (my dad's, before computers, was his stacks of business cards), that card gets dropped into the console of your car, on your desk, or on your dresser at home. Then you likely have a hard time finding it again, right? If you're haphazard in the way you process new contacts, you could be missing out on a powerful new connection or a great relationship in your life.

**IF YOU'RE HAPHAZARD IN THE WAY YOU PROCESS NEW CONTACTS, YOU COULD BE MISSING OUT ON A POWERFUL NEW CONNECTION OR A GREAT RELATIONSHIP IN YOUR LIFE.**

What smart people do (and I hope that includes you) is build a system for bringing those people into their lives. For over two decades now I've used this system: When I get a new business card, I flip the card over, and if it's blank on the back, I write a note or two to help me remember that person. Then I do two things with the card:

1. I have my staff electronically feed the contact's name and information into a software program, so my team and I have it on our phones as well as in our computers. That allows me to effectively keep up with and nourish all the different connections and relationships I have.

2. I have my team put the card in a sleeve on a page in a binder. I have a page for each week, with the year on the spine, and I have binders that go back twenty-plus years. That way I can go back to, say, December of the previous year if I remember that I met someone at a Christmas party that year, and I can find the person I met right there in the binder.

It is crucial that you have a system to collect and organize your connections. Today many people just take a picture of their business cards, and they automatically load into their system. How about you? Are you disorganized about the way you process your connections, or are you one of those really smart people who has a system?

Let me tell you how my current system got started. In 1991 I walked into my office in Las Colinas, and I saw something fascinating. One of my business partners, Ron Lusk, had just bought a brand new Apple Macintosh computer, and his assistant was loading his business cards into a software program on the computer. I was elated. I had been collecting business cards like my dad had taught me to do, and I immediately saw the huge potential for an electronic system. Since then I've been very intentional about hooking up with any new electronic innovation that can multiply my effectiveness with connections—things like e-contact exchanges, LinkedIn, and Facebook.

## THE BENEFITS OF HAVING CONNECTIONS

Recently I authored a book called *Rich Relationships, Rich Life.* That's a great title, isn't it? It's great because it's true. The better your relationships, the better your life. And I'm not talking about just having a list of people you can call to ask a favor. I'm talking about having relationships with people you can help. Think about it. How much are you pouring into the people in your life?

Having the right mindset about relationships really does matter. Zig Ziglar probably impacted my mindset the most in this area. One of his most famous quotes is, **"You can have anything in life you want if you will just help enough other people get what they want."** Are you really living that? If you want to leverage this whole idea about force multiplying through your relationships, helping other people is a big part of that.

Let me tell you about my relationship with Zig. You may remember that I met him on an airplane. Right up front I gave him information that would help him—I explained Chrysler's whole organizational chart to him—and that opened the door for us to develop a great relationship. Over the years I looked for ways I could introduce him to some of the distinctions I'd discovered, and in return he started endorsing my books. That was years ago, and his gift of trust transference—the association of his well-loved and respected name with mine—has been invaluable to me.

Trust transference is one of the most powerful benefits of great relationships. When I was seventeen years old, my grandfather decided to retire from our family's business, and he told me he would carry the financing if I wanted to buy him out. Our family brand was well known in our community, and he had a pristine reputation. He introduced me to all of the people he had great relationships with, and in the process he transferred the trust they had in him to me. That's what I want to do with my kids—transfer that trust over to them. How about you? Wouldn't you like to give the gift of trust transference from your relationships to your kids?

My daughter called me one day about three or four years ago, and she said, "Dad, do you know any executives at Avon or Mary Kay?" Of course she knew the chances were high that I would, because I know tons of people. I said, "Yes, I do. Both of those companies are clients." She said, "I need some free makeup." She went on to explain, "I'm going to be doing a presentation to some underprivileged teenage girls, and I'd like for someone to donate free makeup so I can give these teenagers something that ties into my presentation." I thought that was cool, so I gave her the name of one of my connections at Avon, a super nice lady named Maria. Maria very generously sent her fifty kits of free makeup. My daughter made her presentation and gave the makeup to the teenage girls. Then two or three days later she called me and said, "Dad, I need Maria's address." I said, "What's up?" She said, "I need to handwrite a note to her and thank her for giving me that makeup and impacting those kids' lives." She had learned well.

Here's what happened in that experience: Just as my grandfather transferred the trust from his relationships to me, I was now transferring trust from my relationships to my daughter. When you nourish your connections and do things for them and then are thankful when they do things for you, there is an irrepressible trust that builds up. What a great privilege it is to be able to pass that trust on to your kids! Right? I truly believe that it's not so much about the grades you make as it is about the hands you shake.

Let me tell you about one more thing that impacted my life at an early age. I was exposed to personal development. When I was sixteen years old I read the book *How to Win Friends and Influence People* by Dale Carnegie. If you haven't read it, you probably should. That book is what really started my whole thinking process about turning the lessons I was learning from my dad and my grandfather into a *force multiplier* by listening to and really caring about other people and impacting their lives. Are you serious about doing that with your connections? If you want a happier, more powerful, and more influential life; if you want to grow your career, expand your wins, and leave a legacy, then you need to be more intentionally strategic about your relationships.

> IF YOU WANT A HAPPIER, MORE POWERFUL, AND MORE INFLUENTIAL LIFE; IF YOU WANT TO GROW YOUR CAREER, EXPAND YOUR WINS, AND LEAVE A LEGACY, THEN YOU NEED TO BE MORE INTENTIONALLY STRATEGIC ABOUT YOUR RELATIONSHIPS.

I want you to really own this concept, so I'm going to give you right now nine specific strategies to take action on so you can be your very best.

## NINE KEYS FOR GETTING THE MOST OUT OF YOUR RELATIONSHIPS

1. **Be strategic.** Be strategic about what you want from each and every relationship in your life. Set it up right from the beginning. I live this motto: *Give value, and do more than is expected.* In fact, it's my mantra. I want to give value to every person I touch. Is that something you're thinking about? In every relationship you have, are you thinking about how you can help that person?

When I go to lunch with someone I almost always take a book—most of the time it's one of my books, and sometimes it's a book written by someone else. I like to give away things that will impact people's lives. In fact, when I read a new book that I think is really good, I buy ten of them. I have a shelf in my office where I keep copies of the books I believe will have the most impact on the people in my life, and I stack them in groups of ten. Then when I go to lunch with someone I can pull one of those books off and take it with me. I even autograph other people's books! Maybe you haven't written a book, but you can buy copies of great books and write on the inside cover, "A gift from [your name]." Then you can hand that book to someone and bring value to that person right from the beginning of your relationship. That's being *Intentionally Strategic*.

2. **Be intentional about scheduling time with your relationships.** Schedule time to spend with everyone in your life who is important to you. Put it on your calendar. I enjoy spending time with my mom, and I make that a serious component of my life. I'm intentional about scheduling time with her.

Let me expand your thinking about how that may work. I was having dinner with a friend a few weeks ago, and I was talking about being intentional about spending time with my daughter. He said, "I know I should probably go see my daughter more, but I really don't like going to Ohio." I said, "Why don't you do this: When you're traveling and speaking around the world, why don't you have your daughter and son-in-law travel to meet you?" He said, "That's a great idea! I'm going to do it. You've raised my thinking to a new level there." I encourage you to be intentional about making time to be with those people who are important to you. Rather than not doing it because of some negative component, get creative and make it happen wherever or whenever you can.

3. **Ensure that all stakeholders win.** Let me give you a story about this one right up front. I'm really excited about this. I just bought a brand new Sprinter van. Now, when people fly in to meet with me here in my studio, we'll be able to pick them up at the airport in a

brand new luxury limo that will be decked out like a really nice office. The guy who's building this for me has given me permission to connect with his foreman, whose name is Aaron. I went to meet with Aaron last week, and I said, "Aaron, here's what I'd like to do. I want to build a relationship with you. We can text and send pictures back and forth so you can make this van the way I envision it, and when it's finished I'll give you a bonus. What do you think about that?" He said, "High five! That's great!"

Here's what I was thinking when I made that deal with Aaron: He's a major stakeholder in the three-month process of building this van. The owner, who is also a stakeholder (and I will make sure he wins, as well), has allowed me to connect directly with his foreman instead of sending everything through him. By exchanging pictures and texts directly with Aaron, I can be very specific about what I want while working around my busy schedule. It's a win for both of us.

Boomer, one of my team members, has always wanted to travel to Dubai, so we set a goal last year for him to go. He's a really big win for me and a valuable team member, and I wanted to help him win. So I said to him last Christmas, "Why don't I fly you to Dubai as a Christmas present?" He went to Dubai last month and had a great time. I got a note from his dad a few days later that said, "Thank you for helping my son win."

How about you? Think about all of your relationships. Are you looking at all the different ways you can be creative to make the stakeholders in your life win?

4. **Understand what other people want.** When someone comes to work for me, I ask them to share their goals with me. A while back Bill, one of my mentors, was talking to me about my personal assistant, and he asked, "What's her son's name?" I said, "I don't know." Bill looked at me and said, "You don't know the name of your personal assistant's son?" I said, "Well, obviously she loves her son. She talks about him; however, I don't know his name." Bill said, "One of the things she cares about the most is her son's success, and you should know that. When someone works for you, you need to know what they really want." He was exactly right.

So since that time I've taken this to another whole level. I ask the people around me—those who work for me, the clients I coach, my wife, and my kids—what is important to them. In fact, I go to my kids at the end of each year and ask them, "What are three things you want me to support you in next year?"

Think about that. Wouldn't that be a good thing for you to do? If you have kids, no matter their age, ask them what you can do to support their goals this year. (And that gives you a great opportunity to discuss their goals with them.) You may want to get even more specific and ask what you can do to support them this school year. Understand what other people want. I even list the people I'm closest to in my phone and type in their lists. If you really want to get serious about this, put yours in your phone, as well.

5. **Do *Favors in Advance*.** I'll always remember this one. I was in second grade, and one day I was asked to go to lunch with one of my friends and his dad, who were neighbors. His dad knew I was a real entrepreneurial kid, because I was always selling things, mowing lawns, and doing whatever else I could to make money. He knew I would have cash in my pocket, and he asked me if I wanted to pay for lunch. (Looking back, I know he was joking.) And I thought, *What? I'm a seven-year-old kid and you're an adult. You should be paying for lunch.* I was so stunned I didn't even answer him. In all these years, that has never left my mind. I've thought so many times, *Wow! What if I had paid for lunch? How powerful would that have been?*

Since that time I've been really open to buying lunch for people. You may be thinking, *I don't know if I want to do that, Tony. That's $20 or $30 here and $50 there.* Maybe you want to do a small favor, and it doesn't even have to be something you pay for. For example, how about doing favors for people by connecting them to great URLs? If you're into health like I am and someone says, "Can you help me be healthier?" you can say, "Sure! I'll send you three URLs. If you'll watch the videos on these websites, they can be very valuable to you."

Think about your new relationships. How can you do *Favors in Advance* for them? Maybe you can tap them into some of the best books you've read. As a matter of fact, I have a list of my top 100 books, and I give that list to people as a *Favor in Advance*. (If you would like a copy, e-mail me at info@tonyjeary.com and I'll send you a copy.)

Doing *Favors in Advance* is a powerful way to build up a mental bank account with your relationships. And whether you ever need a favor from them or not, it's a way for you to nourish the people in your life, whether you pay for a lunch, give them a gift, or just do something small that can impact their lives.

6. **Leverage personality styles.** In the last chapter I told you about the book my good friend Dr. Robert Rohm and I wrote together called *Presenting with Style*. Dr. Rohm has taught me to understand and appreciate people's personality styles. If you really want to leverage your relationships, communicate and connect with people the way they want it.

Some people have a direct style, and they're very results-oriented. They want everything to be fast-paced, and they just want to see the bottom line. Don't give someone like that all the details and drag things out; just give them the bottom line up front.

If someone is an influencer and you get down to the bottom line too quickly and don't socialize with them, you're probably missing a connection in that relationship.

Someone who is very steady wants to know where they're going. You can help this person by showing them the steps and how the choices will lead you together.

Other people are very compliant, cautious, and detail-oriented. If you have someone like that in your life, communicate the details and give that person time to digest them. That's where my wife is. She really likes details, she likes to be specific, and she likes fairness. One of the things I do my best in our relationship is understand that about her.

Make sure you understand the specific styles of the people in your life and communicate accordingly.

7. **Identify your POIs.** POIs (*People of Influence*) are those who can have the most impact on our lives and results, both personally and professionally. Your POIs may be customers or clients, they may

be key team members, they may be a coach or a mentor, or they may be friends or family members. Identify the top ten, fifteen, or twenty people who have the most influence over your success, and then take the time to understand what their priorities and goals are. That puts you in a position to nurture them and make sure they're winning, and creating wins for them inevitably creates wins for you somewhere down the line. Keep in touch with them often, send them a card or gift on their birthday, and be sure to do *Favors in Advance*.

Knowing who your *People of Influence* are gives you a remarkable advantage. I want to encourage you to list your POIs in your phone, along with their goals and ambitions and how they want you to support them. Please make sure you get this one down. This is being strategic, and it takes some effort. I teach my high achievers to do this, because it is such a huge piece of getting results faster.

> IN ALL OF YOUR NEGOTIATIONS, ASK YOURSELF, *HOW DO I LOOK AT BOTH (ALL) SIDES AND TRULY MAKE IT A WIN/WIN FOR BOTH OF US?*

8. **Have a true partnership mentality**. So many people miss this. If they're only thinking about what they want when they're negotiating some type of business opportunity, then they're not thinking win/win. It is so powerful when I bring a client on and *they* talk about how *I* can win. Many people don't think this way. When I'm doing a keynote speech for a client somewhere, for example, it's much better for me if I could present it early in the morning so I can get on a plane and fly to wherever I'm going next. If they put me in the middle of the day, that burns the whole day for me. When my client understands that and schedules according to my priorities, it creates a true partnership for both of us. We both win. Look for ways you can pour into other people, not just how you can get the most out of your relationship.

In all of your negotiations, ask yourself, *How do I look at both (all) sides and truly make it a win/win for both of us?*

9. **Be focused on your most common relationships.** Here is a list of fourteen important relationships you may have:

1. Spouse
2. Parents
3. Son/Daughter
4. Siblings
5. Subordinate
6. Client/customer
7. Friend
8. Neighbor
9. Business colleague
10. Leader (Boss/Sponsor)
11. Advisor (Coach, Mentor)
12. Banker, CPA
13. Investors
14. Partners

I encourage you to be clear on who they are. Write them down—who they are and what specific things you can do for those closest to you. Nurture these relationships. Take good care of them.

There you have my big nine. Let me remind you to be *Intentionally Strategic* with your relationships and build the benefits I talked about earlier. Then utilize all nine of these for getting the most out of your relationships, and you'll end up with richer relationships and a rich life.

Before we go on to talk about tools and the impact they can have on your success, I have a bonus for you—the tenth key to getting the most out of your relationships, and it's a big one: Use wisdom and discernment about who you spend time with. If you really want to use your relationships as a force multiplier, you must make sure you hang with the right people, and that includes those you eat dinner with, those you travel with, those you do business with, and those you just hang out with. You really do become who you hang with.

Now let's talk about how tools can be a force multiplier in your life, both personally and professionally.

# Tools

This quote from Bernard Baruch makes sense: "If all you have is a hammer in your tool box, everything looks like a nail." We need to make sure we have all the right tools in our toolbox to give us leverage.

How big is your tool box? And more importantly, how intentional are you in terms of building, maintaining, and utilizing your tool box?

Tools give you leverage, because you can do more if you use the right tools, and you can do it faster. Let me share a story with you. A CEO came into my studio about three years ago, and the number one thing he took away was my Home Depot. Let me explain.

This guy is a very successful business owner, and I have been coaching him for several years—shaping his world, helping him think about his life/kids, and of course teaching him how to really maximize his business. That day I happened to give him a tour of my estate. When we reached my workshop, I showed him my giant tool chest, which I call my mini Home Depot. My workshop actually does have at least one of everything, and sometimes two or six of everything, that you could possibly use to run an estate like mine. He said, "Wow! You do have your own Home Depot!" I never want to run out of anything. If a sprinkler goes out, I want to have one to replace it; if I need a rake, I have it. It includes every tool I could ever need. He said, "I have to take a picture of this toolbox." And that really stuck in my mind—the power of being prepared. My family and I, and even the clients who fly in to my studio, get to enjoy and experience the estate we have here because I leverage a great toolbox.

And that applies to all areas of your life. Having great tools really does matter. Tools help you focus, and they help you execute. Tools also provide consistency.

Using the right tools when you need to cascade things down to your team can be very powerful. Let me give you an example. Ricky Richardson, the president of TGI Friday's, connected with me a few years ago. He said, "Tony, I'd like for you to be my coach." I love this guy. He is so into being the best. He was already fantastic, and he wanted to go to the next level!

Ricky had six points he wanted to cascade down through his organization, and at the time there were about 900 TGI Friday's stores around the world. I shared with him a tool I've used with several top clients called a challenge coin. It's a coin that is commonly used in the military with the organization's insignia on it, and it was originally used to prove membership when challenged (thus the name "challenge coin") or to improve morale. These customized coins have now become popular for businesses to use to reward outstanding performance or mark years of service, or as a way to promote new products, services, or brands. My personal coin is called a Results Coin, and I hand them out to my team members, selected clients, and even to selected top audience members when I do a keynote.

We designed a coin for my client with the TGI Friday's logo, and we put three of the points he wanted to cascade on one side of the coin and three on the other. He had the coin produced and then passed them down to his managers. That one tool was really instrumental in driving clarity to his whole organization to a higher level.

Another client came to me a few years ago and said, "We want you to help us build our culture. We love the whole results faster and *Strategic Acceleration* concept. Can you please help us?" One of the things I talked to them about was building an at-a-glance tool, which is a tool that my organization, TJI, has developed that lists on one page the organization's vision statement, mission statement, tagline, promise, values, standards, goals and objectives, critical success factors, and HLAs. They took that tool and incorporated it into a brochure that showcased their brand and some of their top priorities, which would help their customers and, most importantly, new recruits understand who they were. So instead of taking weeks or months to learn what the company was about, a new person coming on board could look at that one brochure and see in a glance what made the company tick.

Now I'm going to tell you about some selected tools you can use to help you get results faster.

# Five Types of Tools to Accelerate Your Results

1. **Your phone.** You have to get this. All through the book I've been encouraging you to use your phone for more than just talking, e-mailing or texting. Use the notes feature to list:

- Your goals—not just what you want to have, but what you want to share, experience, give, and of course become.

- Your HLAs. Remember, the number one takeaway from this entire book is to be *Intentionally Strategic* about your *High Leverage Activities;* so make sure you write down your HLAs, both personal and professional.

- Your to-do list. You want to be able to look at your to-do list throughout the day and ask yourself, *What's the best use of my time right now?* Determine what items you can mark off in the time you have. Some should be tactical, and some should be strategic.

- Your daily performance standards.

- Your spouse's goals. If you happen to be married, write down the things that are important to your spouse.

- Your kids' goals. Again, if you happen to have kids or grandkids, write down what's important to them.

- Your POIs. List their goals and what's important to them, along with ways you can support them.

2. **Marketing tools.** Great marketing tools give you powerful leverage. I want to encourage you to make sure you take that to the highest level. Let me give a couple of examples.

Fifteen years ago I was on an airplane. One of my first books had just come out, called *Inspire Any Audience.* I was proud of the book, and I was giving a few of them out in first class. As we were getting off the plane, a guy walked up to me on the jet bridge and he said, "Hey, I noticed you were giving away a book to a few people. I sure would like to have one." So I opened my briefcase and got one out and handed it to him. He said, "Wow! At New York Life we really need some help with presentations." He said, "Why don't you come over and visit with me sometime?" I didn't really know who the guy was, so I said, "Sure. Let's talk." So I had someone on my team call him, and it sounded like there was probably a good opportunity for us to connect. I got on the phone and he said, "I want you to come over at 5:30 in the morning." I said, "5:30?" I thought, *This guy is a little strange.* Come to find out, he was one of the top four or five people in New York Life, which was a 150-year-old company at the time, and he was just serious about making things happen. We connected and started developing what turned out to be a great relationship. Because of that book, New York Life ended up investing hundreds of thousands of dollars with me, and it may even be in the millions by now. I handed him the one tool I had available, and it connected us for years.

The very same thing happened again five years ago. I gave a couple of books away when I was on the airplane. (This one happened to be my signature title, *Strategic Acceleration.*) Again, as I was on the jet bridge leaving the plane, a woman said to me, "Hey, I didn't get one of these books." I said, "No problem," and I got one out and handed it to her. She said, "Guess what? I'm building the Success University for HP University right now, and this is perfect." I said, "Cool!" So when I got on the phone with her a couple of days later I discovered that she was making *Strategic Acceleration* the foundation for their entire university! And once again, all because I had that tool to hand to her, it led to an ongoing relationship with many wins for both of us.

Now, of course I believe and have proved that *Strategic Acceleration* is a powerful methodology, and the book is a great tool that anyone would want, right? The point is, you need to think about the marketing tools you have in your life. Do you have them available to you at all times for easy access, and are you using them? Don't be cheap! Give things away. You never know where it will lead.

3. **Self-awareness tools.** These are tools that will make you sharper and help you understand yourself better. We've already talked about some of these in previous chapters.

• SWOT, which is an assessment of four things: your strengths, weaknesses, opportunities, and threats. Many people do a SWOT on their company or on their department, and I'm suggesting you do a SWOT on yourself. Assess those four things and write down your answers in your phone. Then I suggest you go back once or twice a year and look again at your strengths, weaknesses, opportunities, and threats and ask yourself, *Am I really exploiting my strengths? Am I uncovering and sharpening my weaknesses? Am I really taking my opportunities to the highest level and getting better? And am I making sure I cover for any threats?*

- Branding Matrix. Do you have a tool that helps you identify who you want to become? (If this is something you need, e-mail me at info@tonyjeary.com for a free template.)

- MOLO. Do you have in your phone an assessment of what you want more of and what you want less of?

4. **Documented business acumen**. I developed a model when I was working heavily in Japan years back that matches brand with marketing and sales. So many companies don't have those three things aligned. That model is part of my business acumen that I share with others. Look for other models and processes that are out there and save articles and publications that you want to share. Summarize the great books you read and share those summaries. Have documented business acumen in your tool chest that you can share with others, and that can refresh and organize yourself as well.

> PEOPLE REALLY WANT TO RECIPROCATE WHEN YOU GIVE THEM SOMETHING OF VALUE OVER AND ABOVE WHAT THEY WERE EXPECTING.

5. **Giveaways**. Robert Cialdini wrote an exceptional book called *Influence* that talks about the reciprocal principle. People really want to reciprocate when you give them something of value over and above what they were expecting. This is a powerful principle, and I encourage you to build on it.

Have you ever wondered why waiters give you candy when they give you the check? It's because their tip goes up. Studies have shown that because of that one little piece of candy, people give bigger tips. It's human nature. People want to reciprocate.

As I mentioned earlier, you don't have to give things away that cost money. You can give away lists of URLs or great YouTube videos, for example. Just make sure you build your tool chest so you have things to give away.

Start today building your own arsenal of tools so you can go to a whole new level. Keep your tools everywhere. Make sure you can access them and make sure you use them. Enjoy and leverage every tool.

In the next chapter we're going to talk how you can use all the strategies and skills we've talked about in the book to have a big impact on others—through leadership.

# V.I.P.s

- Prepare, prepare, prepare!

- "What can I do to be ready?" is a powerful question we should be asking ourselves all the time.

- It really is about who you know when you want to make things happen faster.

- If you want a happier, more powerful, and more influential life; if you want to grow your career, expand your wins, and leave a legacy, then you need to be more intentionally strategic about your relationships.

- Tools work! The stronger your tool chest (arsenal), the faster you'll get results.

- Tools help you focus, they help you execute, and they provide consistency.

# CHAPTER 6:

# LEADERSHIP

Now that you're armed with the *Strategic Acceleration* formula and three powerful force multipliers that will significantly enhance your efforts as you put the formula to work, let's see how it all plays out in taking your leadership to the next level.

Here's my definition of leadership: **A leader is one who sets a clear vision and shares that vision with others so they can willingly focus their efforts to ensure execution of the vision with the right information, resources, and methods.**

As we introduce the topic of leadership, I'm going to do something a little different. When I bring top achievers and leaders of all kinds into my private studio, I start out with an assessment of where they are as a leader. I call the assessment my Leadership 25. These are not the only important leadership qualities, of course. However, these are twenty-five very powerful characteristics that I've built into this framework from working with many of the top executives around the world. They are organized into five key areas of focus: Focus and Clarity, Personal Development, Presentation/Communication, Leading a Strong Team, and People Power.

I want to give you the benefit of my Leadership 25 assessment here. So I encourage you to get out a piece of paper and number it 1 to 25, and then rate yourself on each characteristic on a scale of one to four, with one being the lowest and four being the highest. Feel free to use the half marks if they are applicable (1.5, 2.5, and 3.5).

## FOCUS AND CLARITY

1. **Strategic planning.** How strategic are you? Do you have a powerful and well-thought-out strategic plan tied to a simple, well-thought-out vision? And do you have a system for ensuring all team members understand the vision and are reminded of it constantly to ensure focus?

2. **Vision model/tools.** Do you utilize visual representation or tools to complement your plan and vision that will help your team understand where you're going? It could be a picture, card, magnet, coin, poster, or even a screen saver.

3. **SWOT/MOLO.** Do you assess your strengths and weaknesses and what you want to do more of and less of two or three times a year? Top leaders assess themselves so they can double down on their identified strengths and shore up areas that need attention.

4. **Benchmarking.** How well do you benchmark yourself, your organization, and your team? Do you look around you, modeling part or all of the best to grow your effectiveness?

5. **Competitive/comparison.** As a leader are you keeping up with your competition? Are you and the people on your team serving up what's going on with the competition so you can see trends, sweet spots, and industry best practices?

## PERSONAL DEVELOPMENT

6. **Professional brand.** Do you have a strategic approach to your

brand (reputation) inside and outside of your organization, including your reputation with investors, new team members, all departments, and of course your clients and customers?

7. **Health and energy management**. As a leader, are you on top of your diet, timing, stress, and even your sleep? It's not just about 168 hours in a week; it's about being at your peak for top opportunities.

8. **Feeding your mind**. Are you growing and learning? And you reading and listening? Are you being coached so you consistently model self-improvement for those you lead? Are you avoiding stagnation with constant, fresh inputs?

> IT'S NOT JUST ABOUT 168 HOURS IN A WEEK; IT'S ABOUT BEING AT YOUR PEAK FOR TOP OPPORTUNITIES.

9. **Stress management**. As a leader you have to remain calm and cool. Are you leveraging exercise, stretching, relaxation, and rest to help you stay physically and mentally fit and manage your stress?

10. *Strategic Presence*. Are you looking sharp and up to date, and are you being admired for your wardrobe and grooming?

A number of years ago I recognized the power of always looking sharp, so I started hiring people to help me look at my grooming and wardrobe. I discovered secrets like buying a belt two inches bigger than my waist, which helps you look slimmer. I learned to be crisp with my wardrobe by having my clothes tailored to fit my body. All those pieces really do matter with your *Strategic Presence*.

## PRESENTATION/COMMUNICATION

11. **Meeting effectiveness**. Are you making sure that your meetings really are necessary? And when they are, do they include good objectives and a strong agenda? Are the right people there? And do you include good, clear actions at the end of each meeting?

12. *Presentation Universe.* Are you effectively managing all of your presentations? Think about all the different presentations you give and

how well you manage them. Do you prepare well?

13. **Personality profiling**. Do you understand and utilize profiling tools (like DISC, for example) for all hiring, motivating, and negotiating? Do you know the personalities of the people around you, and are you really communicating with and leading them according to their personalities and preferences?

14. *Presentation Ready.* Have you thought through tools and messaging for both prepared and impromptu presentation opportunities?

15. **Daily huddles.** Do you have a consistent habit of daily calibrating your team—by phone or in person—so you can have synchronized focus and clarity of priorities?

I was in Japan years ago coaching the president of Seiyu Corporation (which was the largest retailer in Japan at the time), and I watched the top executives there do daily ten-minute stand-up huddles around a table, calibrating the top executives of a 400-chain organization. It was impressive.

## Leading a Strong Team

16. **Performance standards**. Do you have written performance standards for yourself and those around you, especially your direct reports, to help ensure expectations are met and that shorten the learning curve for new people joining your team?

17. **Mentoring**. Are you pouring into the people on your team, talking about bench strength and helping them grow?

18. *People of Influence* (**POI**). Are you consistently touching those who have the biggest influence on your objectives? Have you made a list of your POIs and put it in your phone so it will trigger reminders to connect with them on a regular basis?

19. **Advisors**. Do you have a team of advisors who are pouring into your life to help guide and stimulate you and bring fresh ideas and perspectives? Have you surrounded yourself with the right coaches, mentors, trusted colleagues, and paid professionals so you can be on your game?

20. **Culture**. How is your team synergy? Is it improving and really playing out trust and accountability as well as good, open communication?

## PEOPLE POWER

21. **Assistant effectiveness**. Do you have an executive assistant (or multiple assistants) or someone else you can delegate to so they save your time as a leader and allow you to be focused and most impactful with your HLAs?

I have a full checklist of ways your assistant can be of help to you, and I'll give you seven of them here. (If you would like a copy of the full checklist, e-mail me at info@tonyjeary.com.)

- Presentation/communications management
- Office and desk management
- Calendaring, scheduling appointments, and proactive management
- Executive focus and clarity
- Travel/events
- Saving time
- Personal development

22. **Time-saving team**. Do you utilize a driver so you can use your commute time more effectively? Does your team help you with *Smart Reports*? Do they plan your travel and your schedule and help you organize your time so that you're maximizing the things that will bring you the best results faster?

23. **Networking/connections.** Do you have that system we've been talking about for building and nourishing your new and existing connections?

24. **Social capital**. Are you doing *Favors in Advance* for people and building up your social capital?

25. **Stuff Management**. Think about your closets, decks, backpack, and briefcase, the files in your computer, your vehicles, and of course your phone. Are all of these really organized, or do you have clutter? Do you have defined and refined systems and the right people around

you to keep them organized?

So there you have twenty-five specifics that I encourage you to take to heart in order to be an exceptional leader.

Now I'm going to take three of those twenty-five and go deep with them in this chapter. We will have specific segments on your professional brand, persuading people to take action, and team building. Let's get started.

# Your Professional Brand

I want to show you in this section how to heighten your professional brand and leverage it to get extraordinary results, and I'll also be touching on your personal brand, especially as it relates to your family.

**WE ALL HAVE A BRAND. TOP LEADERS ARE STRATEGIC ABOUT BUILDING THEIRS.**

What are you known for? What is your top strength? Most people don't strategically develop their brands; they just let their reputations play themselves out. If you want to be an exceptional leader, I suggest you be strategic about building your brand. A successful brand represents who you are. It's your unique promise. Build a brand based not only on what you want to be and how you want to live, but also who you actually are and the core of how you live today. People want to do things with people they trust and respect. They want to know you will get the job done. They want to know you bring value to their world. The bottom line is this: We all have a brand. Top leaders are strategic about building theirs. Think about your brand and determine how you want to be known. Then build it out and leverage it every way you can.

To help you clarify your personal brand, I'm going to take you through eight elements that define the essence of your brand positioning. When I bring the highest level executives into my private studio, I sit down with them and get them to start thinking about the very things I'm teaching you now. Whether you're a top executive, you lead a team of any kind, you lead a small group, or you just think about yourself as the leader of your family, I want you to think about your brand and how powerful it can be to you as a leader. Having a strong brand makes a big impact.

Before we get into the eight elements, let me just touch on your brand with your kids. Both of my daughters and son-in-law recognize that they are right up there among the things I care about the most, along with God and my wife. I have a strong brand as a parent with my kids. They know that I am the president of their fan clubs. I'm intentional about it, I talk about it, and I am continually building that brand with them. How about you? Does your brand with your kids let them know they are among your top priorities? I want you to really think about that as we go through these eight elements.

## Eight Elements of Brand Positioning

1. **Audience/prospect.** Who will you be targeting your brand to? If you're branding to your prospects or to an audience through a presentation, you need to understand precisely what's important to them and what they value.

2. **Top communication opportunities**. You have many opportunities to build your brand through communication. That may be as you communicate to your board, to your clients, to people you want to recruit, or even to your family members. Or perhaps you have an opportunity to build your brand through film. For some it's through staff meetings, whether you're leading or just participating. When you speak up in a staff meeting, that's a communication opportunity to build your brand. Even sending an e-mail or doing an e-blast is an opportunity to build your brand through communication.

When someone sees an e-mail from you that's succinct and organized into bullets, with a concise yet descriptive subject line, your brand will be speaking to them, saying, "This person is efficient and organized." I'm not saying it has to be perfect; in fact, I don't think you need to take the time to make everything perfect (including spelling) on internal communications. I'm talking about efficiency. If you want efficiency to be part of your brand, people need to see that in every way you communicate.

How about the way you hold meetings? Do you set them up with clear objectives and a strong agenda right up front? Do you tell the participants in the invitation, "These are the three things we want to accomplish [your objectives], and these are the five things we're going to do [your agenda] to make sure that happens"? When you communicate that to your participants

WHEN SOMEONE SEES AN E-MAIL FROM YOU THAT'S SUCCINCT AND ORGANIZED INTO BULLETS, WITH A CONCISE YET DESCRIPTIVE SUBJECT LINE, YOUR BRAND WILL BE SPEAKING TO THEM, SAYING, "THIS PERSON IS EFFICIENT AND ORGANIZED."

before every meeting and then start your meeting by reviewing the objectives and agenda, they know that part of your brand is holding time-efficient meetings. They don't dread your meetings, because they know they're going to be crisp.

3. **Brand description**. I encourage you to write down four to six words in each of these categories:

- Characteristics that do describe you and/or that you'd like to be described by

- Characteristics that do not describe you.

For example, I don't want to be known as lazy. I want people to know that I'm energetic and encouraging, and that I love on people.

4. **What people are missing about you.** Write down any distinctions that people don't really know about, or maybe that people misunderstand about you. As you're building your brand, you need to adjust these characteristics and determine how to make them part of the brand you want to have.

5. **Uniqueness**. Write down three or four qualities that truly make you special. Maybe it's your history. You may have been with a company for a long time, and you have an exceptional understanding of a certain process, or maybe you have a long history in one particular niche, and you're extremely gifted in that particular area.

6. **What people think of you.** Write down three or four words that describe your perception of how people perceive you.

7. **Attributes prized in the workplace (or at home)**. Write down the attributes or qualities you possess that are valued in your organization (or in your home), and include the attributes and qualities you want to be valued for. Who you want to become is important.

8. **Your core value proposition**. What are the core characteristics that are valuable to your effectiveness? I am an encourager, and that is the core characteristic that makes me valuable to my clients. So my core value proposition would be, "I encourage people. I want to support them and bring out the best in them. I am constantly looking at ways to bring more value." Write down the core value proposition that you bring to the world.

As we wrap up, I want to give you one more thing to think about. Are you memorable? What specifically do you want people to remember about you? And I'm not just talking about your brand or your personality. It has more to do with your presence. It's a certain image that causes people to see you as a particular kind of person. Your trademark expression, style, or persona makes you memorable  or not.

Have you ever met someone you just knew was different from everyone else? Maybe they were humorous, carefree, or extremely positive, and you remembered them for that. Or in your case, maybe you're an entrepreneur who values freedom, creativity, and the power to choose, and that's what makes you different from the majority. Maybe you stand out because you do an extraordinary job of making a difference in the lives of others. Whatever makes you memorable and authentically you, embrace it and bring it out in everything you do.

I believe my persona has to do with my energy, my positive attitude, and my over-the-top determination to bring value to others. How about you? How does the world see your presence—your persona?

# PERSUASION

Leaders have to persuade people to take action—period. If no one is taking action, you're not really leading.

Let me tell you, I wasn't always effective at persuading people. My first time on a stage was thirty years ago, in Seattle, Washington, in front of a thousand people. It was my first big speaking gig—a tour of forty cities—and I thought I would be really good. I had done everything I knew to prepare, including renting a hotel room and rehearsing like crazy in front of my coach. I was extremely nervous. In fact, I was so nervous I hadn't even wanted to get on the plane. My coach had had to virtually shove me onto the plane.

So there I was on stage speaking to a thousand people. After a few minutes, I saw one person leave, then another person left, and then another and another. Before long, about fifty people left. I thought, *I'm supposed to be persuading these people, and I can't even keep them in the room.* Then the ones who were still in the room start pointing at me and laughing. I thought, *What? Are my pants unzipped? What's going on with this?* They just kept pointing and laughing, and more people kept leaving.

Come to find out, half of my slides (back then we used cellophane slides) were upside down! Imagine! For thirty minutes I had been talking with upside down slides. That was pretty embarrassing! I'm telling you, that did not feel good!

I bet you've had some embarrassing times, too. We all have, even though yours may not have been quite as bad. The point is, I had to learn to get good at persuasion. After that experience, I stepped back and said, *Every time I get*

**IF YOU WANT TO BE AN EXTRAORDINARY LEADER, YOU HAVE TO BECOME AN EXTRAORDINARY PERSUADER.**

*in front of a room I'm going to get better and better.*

If you want to be an extraordinary leader, you have to become an extraordinary persuader. I've published quite a bit about persuasion. In fact, twenty-six of my forty-five books are on presentations; and of those twenty-six, several of them deal specifically with how to influence people to take action. I want to help you improve your skill sets and techniques so you can more effectively influence people to take action, so this session will include my twelve best principles of effective persuasion.

## TWELVE PRINCIPLES OF PERSUASION

1. **Help others win and be right.** Say you're making a presentation—it could be around the dinner table at a restaurant, or it could be in a big group or a small group—and someone says something that reinforces what you're saying. You could say, "Yeah, you're right," and just keep moving. Or you could say something like, "You know, Bill, you're right. Tell me more." All of a sudden Bill feels good because you called him out and affirmed him. Helping other people win—whether it's your kid or a subordinate or a customer—is something we often overlook. So many people get caught up in being right and appearing strong that they fail to understand the emotions that happen when they let other people win.

Now I'm talking about being genuine here, not fake. If someone really is saying something strong, compliment them and let them win. Tell them they're right, and let them share that feeling of power.

2. **Build a value arsenal to share.** We've talked about the reciprocal principle before, and it really is powerful. When you give something to somebody, they naturally want to give back. That's why there's such value in having an arsenal of things you can easily give to people.

Let me give you an example. In the last five years I've really shaped up my health. When I see people I haven't seen for a while, they say, "Wow! Tony, you've really changed!" I'm always thinking about how I can give value to people, so when someone says that I often give them a book I've written called Ultimate Health. Several years ago I had teamed up with two doctors to put an incredible book together, and it's now part of my value arsenal.

Do you have a good arsenal of things you can share with people? As I mentioned when we talked about this before, you can give away things that don't even cost anything, like lists of URS or YouTube videos, and even book summaries. Whatever you have to give can evoke the reciprocal principle, which often leads to persuasion.

3. **Take stock in who you know.** In Chapter 5 we talked about relationships. Understanding who you know that you can get information from is one important piece of the puzzle. Knowledge is power, so if you want to be more persuasive, get intelligence. Tap into those relationships who know people who know people.

> KNOWLEDGE IS POWER, SO IF YOU WANT TO BE MORE PERSUASIVE, GET INTELLIGENCE. TAP INTO THOSE RELATIONSHIPS WHO KNOW PEOPLE WHO KNOW PEOPLE.

A friend called me a while back who had a person in mind he wanted to hire. In fact, he really wanted to recruit this person. He asked me if I knew him, and I didn't, so I went into LinkedIn, made a couple of connections, and got the intelligence my friend wanted. Armed with that intelligence, he was able to recruit him. And because I was a persuasive person, I was able to give him what he needed.

I get many notes from people saying, "Can you connect me with this or that person?" Because I know many people, I have connections and can make things happen. When the people in my world are looking for a certain person, they know I have influence and can open doors.

How about you? Can you see how taking stock in who you know fits into the puzzle of being more persuasive?

4. **Show people the clear picture.** Here's a story that illustrates this principle: Five years ago my wife and I celebrated our twentieth anni-

versary. I had invested four months developing twenty three-minute videos of the seventy-five or eighty best pictures of each year that we had been married. All together, they made a sixty-minute video. I flew with my wife to Mexico, where we stayed at one of the best hotels in all of the country, called the One&Only Palmilla in Cabo San Lucas. It's a beautiful place. On the way there she was watching the video I had made of our entire life together, and when she got through the ninth year she started crying and couldn't even watch the rest of it. It was really special.

Here's the point of the story: When we got there, we checked into our casita suite, and I immediately saw some flaws. I thought, *This isn't good*, and I started looking around. I saw that right next door there was an even better casita—and it was huge. I thought, *That's the one we want.* So I said to my wife, "This is our twentieth anniversary and I want it to be really nice, so I'm going to the front desk to see what I can do." I went to the front desk and said to the young lady there, "Hey, I was thinking about an upgrade to that casita next door to us. Since there's no one there, may we get an upgrade?" She got on her computer for a few minutes and finally said, "Yes, we can do it." I said, "Great!" She said, "And it will only cost you another $2,200." I knew right then that I hadn't shown her the clear picture. What I wanted was a free upgrade. So I said, "Now, let's talk about this a little more." I said, "You know, this is our twenty-year wedding anniversary. I know tons of people, I'm a Centurion® Member, and I plan to really brag about your place. I was wondering if you could give us a free upgrade. Would you please go talk to your hotel manager and see if you can do that?" So she did, and she walked back into the room a few minutes later with her thumbs up and a big smile on her face. She

> **WHEN YOU WANT TO BE PERSUASIVE, MAKE SURE YOU GIVE PEOPLE THE CLEAR PICTURE. WALK THEM THROUGH THE STEPS OF EVERY SINGLE THING YOU WANT TO HAPPEN.**

said, "He'll do it!"

Now the whole point is this: When I finally gave her the clear picture, it made it happen. So when you want to be persuasive, make sure you give people the clear picture. Walk them through the steps of every single thing you want to happen.

5. **Discover and be aware of what others really want.** I've said this in other chapters, and I'm saying it again because I want you to get it. When people are part of your life, understand what they really want. If you're not sure, ask them. When you're presenting to one or more people in an organization, be careful about presenting to a company. Companies don't buy; people do. You need to make sure you discover what the people want.

6. **Figure out what you really want, down to the smallest detail.** When you go into a new relationship, like a partnership or joint venture, or when you recruit someone into your organization, or even when you get married, don't you want to really figure out what you want in that relationship so you can have a reciprocal understanding? When you make a deal with a client, don't you want to know what you want out of it, down to the smallest detail? And don't you want the same thing for them?

When I send an e-mail to my informal board, where we trade ideas and insights with each other, and I ask for them to e-mail me back with their distinctions, just like I do for them, I'm really clear about what I want. You're in a better position to persuade when you're really clear on what you want.

7. **Labeling**. This is one of my favorites. Label people what you want them to become. If someone works for you and they're very organized, call them organized, and they'll want to continue to live up to that. That's a powerful aspect of persuasion.

I call my oldest daughter a cheerleader. That's her label. She actually grew up cheering and became a national cheer champion. I noticed early on that she was a natural, and I wanted her to take that bubbly personality—her name is Brooke—and go out into the world and cheer people on.

We were on an Alaskan cruise two years ago to take my parents-in-law on an envisioned trip of a lifetime, and this cruise had many older people on board. Now, my wife and I are not in that group, and neither are my kids, of course. (We still enjoyed the cruise.) We were attending a performance one night, and the performers were late. I looked over, and there was my daughter, standing up and looking back at the audience and cheering them on. Now remember, there were quite a few older people in the room, and she was having them do all kinds of things to keep the atmosphere positive. She was really in the moment and was just loving on people. I could definitely see the influence I'd had in her life by labeling her.

My youngest daughter is a champion, and that's what I labeled her. She's been a champion at just about any sport she's ever tried. She was a champion in school. And now, everywhere she goes she makes champions out of the people she leads.

**WHEN YOU LABEL PEOPLE, THEY MENTALLY OWN THE NAME, AND THEY WANT TO LIVE UP TO IT.**

So think about the people in your life. Do you have a label for your spouse and for your kids? Do you have a label for the people that work for you? For your boss? When you label people, they mentally own the name, and they want to live up to it. This is a very powerful piece to the persuasion puzzle.

8. **Leverage social proof**. Use testimonials. People do what other people do. If you don't have good testimonials, stories, and case studies, you're missing out. If I were to tell you that the president of Walmart flew his jet to Dallas to sit down with me to strategize his plan (which he did), you would think, *Wow! If Tony's good enough for the president of the largest company in the world, maybe he's good enough for me.* Social proof is powerful. Make sure that you leverage it.

9. **Be flexible and communicate in the style the recipient wants to receive your message.** I've said this several times in this book, and I'll keep saying it because it's so powerful. Make sure you manage your

pace. If someone's quick, go faster. If they're a little slower, maybe you need to relax your pace. If they want a ton of details and you're pretty high-level, slow down and give them the details. Be flexible and communicate to people the way they want it. Do it their way—not yours!

10. **Be a storyteller.** Years ago my business manager, who had been with me for many years, told me that I needed to be really good at storytelling. I resisted it for a while, and that was a mistake. I don't want you to make the same mistake. I want you to start ramping up your storytelling skills now. When you hear something or experience something, log it in your mind as a story you can use to engage people. People are persuaded when you paint the picture so they can get the point. Help them understand by reliving what you're sharing with them.

> GIVE VALUE;
> DO MORE THAN
> IS EXPECTED.

11. **Exceed expectations**. My mantra, as I've shared with you before, is to give value and do more than is expected. Always be thinking, *Give value; do more than is expected.* If you exceed expectations with the people you come in contact with, you will have more influence and persuasion. And constantly giving value is a reputation we all want to have.

12. **Preempt objections**. No matter who you're trying to persuade, think through the toughest questions they may have and prepare the best responses. Whether you're talking to your neighbor or your spouse or your kids, you're negotiating a deal, you're recruiting someone to an organization, or you're talking to a customer or client, think about any objections they could have that would cause them not to say yes. And then be ready with the best response that will make it easy for them to say yes.

I was working with the president of a large organization recently, and he was getting ready to do a group presentation about his company to a specific group of analysts. I thought the analysts would probably direct objections at him, and I knew he needed to be ready. I was pretty sure there would be objections to his vision, and there were.

We had prepared responses in advance, and he and his team were able to really communicate the fundamentals back to their audience. This session was being recorded and was going all over the world, and he had a big win because he was prepared and ready with the answers to those objections ahead of time.

Let me just mention as we wind this segment down that about half of the twelve principles on persuasion I've shared with you are about helping others win. Please get this point: Help others win. Being genuine trumps everything. Be real, and really care.

# Team Building

This section is about the incredible leverage that comes from tapping into the power of building exceptional teams.

You may remember I mentioned earlier in the book that in 1995, when I was coaching the president of Ford, they gave me a million dollars and commissioned me to do a special team–building project for their top executives. I wasn't a team-building expert at the time; yet because they trusted me and my brand—being a person who made things happen—I got the assignment. I poured a year of my life into understanding the difference between a group and a team, and I learned how to bring people together into a *High-Performing Team*. Since that time I've positively impacted many organizations with this expertise—company after company—and proved it out, and I'm going to share it with you now.

Let me start out by giving you the incredible benefits of leveraging team synergy:

- It uses collective intelligence and expertise. When we were in my studio recording the videos for the *RESULTS Faster!* online course that complements this book, we had about fifteen people supporting us to make that special experience for our viewers, and we were tapping everyone's years of expertise as a team to bring it all together. The result was a powerful course—and this book—that will help people all over the world accelerate their results. It was a beautiful experience to watch the team's synergy bring the best of my life's work together and make it happen.

- It expands leadership. If you're concerned about bench strength, team synergy allows you to mentor people more and bring them up.

- It supports training and cross-training, where people learn from each other.

- It promotes fantastic employee/team engagement and enjoyment. We all feel good when we're part of a winning team.

- Execution is improved; hence, results happen. With team synergy, everyone benefits.

Now let's take a look at the characteristics of a *High-Performing Team*, and then I'm going to give you the three very best things you can do as a leader to make a *High-Performing Team* a reality for you.

First let's look at my model, where we see the difference between a group, a team, and a *High-Performing Team*. As we go through this, think about your own organization, whether you have six people or six hundred, and see where you fit in this model.

Level one in the model is the group. In a group, the people work with no common goals or tasks, and each person executes their tasks independently. They may do fairly well in their silos and be able to make things happen, and yet they really aren't synergized. Many organizations function at this level, where their people are in groups and not part of a team.

Level two is the team. It's a group of people working together interdependently toward a common goal. A team is one level above a group, and yet it still is not the top level.

> **A *HIGH-PERFORMING TEAM* WORKS TOGETHER TO GET THE VERY BEST RESULTS, AND THEY CONTINUALLY REEVALUATE TO MAKE SURE THEY PRODUCE THE BEST QUALITY.**

Where you really want to be is level three, and that's operating as a *High-Performing Team*. At this level, your people are focused on being as effective as possible. They work together to get the very best results, and they continually reevaluate to make sure they produce the best quality. Each team member has a high level of investment in the outcomes, so each individual is highly motivated. That's a *High-Performing Team*. Don't get stuck in leading a group or a team. Take it to the highest level—a *High-Performing Team*.

I think you know what that feels like. Remember all the way back in grade school, or in high school or college, when you were on some type of team where everyone was really synergized and working together? It felt really good, didn't it? Everyone was humming together, and there were so many wonderful wins. A *High-Performing Team* is where you really want to go to be able to execute at the highest level.

So now you want to be at that level, and you're saying, "How do I make that happen?" I've found that there are three powerful elements that make the difference in moving up through those levels: accountability, communication, and trust.

## Keys to Building a High-Performing Team: A.C.T.

1. **Accountability**. People do what they say they're going to do, on time or before. When someone drops the ball here, what happens to your team synergy? It goes down. If someone says a task needs to be done by noon and by noon it's done, the synergy goes up. If someone says it needs to be done by noon and it's not there until two o'clock, the synergy goes down. If you can't do something on time, you may have to renegotiate your commitment. There's no problem with that; sometimes that needs to happen. And sometimes things that get done are not going to be perfect. However, if you don't communicate that and renegotiate it, guess what? The synergy goes down. Accountability is what keeps synergy going.

And measuring the results with consistent outputs is so powerful for a High-Performing Team. Watching and making sure you've done what you said you were going to do and putting that "x" in the box makes the team synergy go up, and accountability happens.

2. **Communication**. One of the top ten standards in my own organization is to over-communicate. I sometimes even double or triple an e-mail to make sure everyone has the message. You're probably saying, "That's not very efficient." Well, we're just making sure nothing falls through the cracks. We know the power of communication.

Communication starts with the vision, where you're going. I had a group in here just a few weeks ago, and we were talking about taking the executive team to the highest level. We recognized pretty quickly that there was a challenge from a communication standpoint. The owners of the organization had not defined the mission and vision for the executive management team. Because there was no real clarity about the mission and vision for the organization, they were struggling and were not able to synergize at the highest level as a team. Let me encourage you, as a leader, to ensure the vision and mission are clearly understood and cascaded all the way down in your organization. Make sure you're using the right tools to communicate to your people—a vision board, standards, cards, or even the coin I mentioned earlier.

And finally, make sure your meetings are clear, maximized, and inspiring. We've thoroughly covered this topic in other parts of this chapter, and we mention it again here because it is so vital for leaders to have effective meetings with defined objectives and strong agendas if they want to take their organizations to the highest level.

> WITH A CULTURE OF TRUST, INDIVIDUAL EXPERTISE IS VALUED AND RESPECTED, SUPPORT IS GIVEN, INNOVATION HAPPENS, AND TEAM MEMBERS ARE EMPOWERED.

3. **Trust**. People on your team will follow through if there's a high level of trust. With a culture of trust, individual expertise is valued and respected, support is given, innovation happens, and team members are empowered. Because

of the synergy that comes with trust, expectations are managed very carefully. If someone says they're going to do something, they usually do it. You want to have a team where trust is maintained and people do what they're supposed to do, and on time.

You can remember my three keys for building a *High-Performing Team* by just remembering the mnemonic A.C.T.—accountability, communication, and trust. And speaking of A.C.T., here are three actions I encourage you to take to build a team that's performing at the highest level of accountability, communication, and trust:

1. Understand that you need to build from groups to teams, and then to *High-Performing Teams.* Communicate to your people the difference in those levels and make sure they understand where you're headed. Show them the benefits of a *High-Performing Team* that we bulleted out at the beginning of this section. Persuade them to jump on board with you, because they can all win as part of a *High-Performing Team.*

2. Recognize and reward team performance rather than just individual achievements. That means if people are doing fantastic things as a team, acknowledge that and express your appreciation to them as a team. One of the things I encourage my clients to do when I go into an organization is establish pooled bonuses. If the entire team comes together and accomplishes something together, they're rewarded with a bonus that is tied to that team win.

Remember, you get more of what you appreciate, so appreciate your team's synergy. If the team is doing something outstanding together, send out an e-mail to every person on the team and let them know how much you appreciate their working together. Acknowledge their wins. Promote them as a team at every opportunity.

Post pictures of the team synergy. One of my personal goals is to have team synergy among my family members. So for the last fifteen years I have strategically taken pictures of my family functioning as a team, such as high-fiving each other and doing fun things together, so we could constantly relive the whole idea of working as a team.

How about you? As a leader, do you verbally appreciate the entire team when the team has a really good win together?

3. Show trust (and recognize employees' abilities). When your team knows they can trust you and that you will recognize their abilities, they're motivated to go the extra mile. Improve your bench strength by investing time in mentoring them, and be sure you're genuine in your relationship with them. Prove you want to help them win by providing the right training for them to reach their goals.

Let me leave you with a powerful exercise you can do with your family or your team at work to create and build synergy. I call it the appreciation exercise.

Imagine this. You're attending a meeting at work with fifteen or twenty people (it doesn't really work with more than twenty), or you're having dinner with your family at home. You hand everyone there a three-by-five card and ask each person to write their name on the top of the card and then pass it to the person on their right. When the cards have been passed, ask them to write down one or two things they appreciate about the person whose name is on the card and then pass the card to the person on their right. Repeat the process, so that every person writes something on everyone's card. When the cards get back to the original owner, that person reads out loud what the others have written.

**APPRECIATION TAKES TEAM SYNERGY TO ANOTHER LEVEL, BECAUSE EVERYONE LOVES TO BE APPRECIATED.**

This is really an extraordinary exercise that takes team synergy to another level, because everyone loves to be appreciated. And you as the leader can foster that.

Doing this exercise in your own family is powerful. If you want to do it without cards, you can just have them look at each other in rotation and say, "Here's one thing I appreciate about you." It's a wonderful exercise for a family.

I've given you quite a bit to think about, and I hope you put these best practices to work in your journey to becoming the best leader you can be. Now it's time to take everything you've learned up to the highest level—the level of mastery—to give you the ultimate results you've always dreamed about.

# V.I.P.s

- Your strategic presence or your brand has a unique impact on how people will follow your lead. Make it strong.

- Think strategically about your brand and determine how you want to be known. Then build it out and leverage it every way you can.

- Extraordinary leadership must include extraordinary influence, when it comes to getting people to take action.

- Many of the principles of persuasion have to do with helping others win. Your influence multiplies when you help others get what they want.

- There are three magic keys to building a *High-Performing Team:* accountability, communication, and trust.

- A *High-Performing Team* works together to get the very best results, and they continually reevaluate to make sure they produce the best quality.

# CHAPTER 7:

# Mastery

Mastery is the final step of the RESULTS Faster! experience. You know, I want you to tap into and really get Clarity, Focus, and Execution. I want you to latch on to the multipliers we talked about. I want you to go to another level in your leadership. And I also want you to live in mastery. **Don't stop at greatness. Many people do. I want you to go all the way to mastery**, and I'm ready to take you there right now.

First, I want to share with you a very powerful quote by James Michener. When I first read this quote, I had to read it over and over. In fact, I put it in my phone so I could read it yet over and over again. Here it is: "The master in the art of living makes little distinction between his work and his play, his labor and his leisure, his mind and his body, his information and his recreation, his love and his religion. He hardly knows which is which. He simply pursues his vision of excellence at whatever he does, leaving others to decide whether he's working or playing. To him, he's always doing both."

That is powerful! When I read it, I immediately thought, *You know, that's where I want to play.* And my real desire is to help you play there as well.

One thing I've learned in working with so many top achievers all over the world is this: *The biggest enemy of mastery is greatness.* Many

## THE BIGGEST ENEMY OF MASTERY IS GREATNESS.

people live at the good level. Some live at the great level. Very few, however, move past that and get to the mastery level. Mastery is a puzzle that requires the right pieces, and I'm going to give you three of those pieces right now. These are three of my very top distinctions that can tip the scale for you in your climb to mastery: clear standards, a strong *Life Team*, and powerful habits.

**Standards**. Most people have never taken the time to document standards for themselves and/or their organizations. They may say they have them, yet few have documented them. I'm going to take you through a step-by-step process of how to really look at your own personal standards, and then to develop standards for the people in your life, family, team, or organization.

**Life team**. One of my favorite distinctions of living in mastery is building and nourishing a *Life Team*. Often when I share this concept with people, they have a real "aha" moment, and I hope it's that for you as well. Here's a question I get over and over: "Tony, how do you get so much done? How do you write all these books, do all these courses, serve all of these high-profile clients, and still have such a fantastic family life, live so healthily, and enjoy the world?" And here's my answer: my *Life Team*.

In this section, I'm going to talk about really zeroing in on helping the people who are part of your *Life Team* win as they help you have an exceptional life and execute so you get more results. I'll be sharing many of the personal things I do that that you may want to duplicate. When I'm coaching people right here in my studio, they love it when I go deep on this one and share my personal distinctions, and I'm going to do that for you as well.

**Habits**. We all know that our habits should be good, and yet most people don't look specifically at the habits they should develop. They spend more time focusing on the habits they should eliminate. We're going to look at both, and then I'll give you a powerful exercise that will show you the importance of not focusing on eliminating the negative habits, and instead, focusing on replacing them with habits that will help move you to the mastery level.

Remember, the belief that greatness already exists in your life becomes the enemy of mastery. Let's get started.

# Standards

I'm going to be very serious with you about this distinction. If you want to advance to or go further up into the mastery level, you have to get this distinction right. Period. Cultures are built around standards. Standards really do matter at the highest level.

We're going to talk about both personal standards and professional standards. We all have them, though most people are not strategic enough to write them down. The benefits from doing that are endless, and I want to help you get it right.

MANY OF THE BEST OPPORTUNITIES HAPPEN WHEN THE PEOPLE AT THE TOP HAVE THEIR STANDARDS DOCUMENTED.

As you know by now, I've worked with some of the brightest people in the world—people who have run extremely successful enterprises of all different kinds. One thing I've found most interesting is that many of the best opportunities happen when the people at the top have their standards documented.

Let me explain. You see, I strongly believe people at the top want the people in their organizations below them to know how they think. And that includes anyone who joins their team, whether it's large or small. For the most part leaders at the top have gone through plenty of things, figured out plenty, and have developed personal systems and processes that work. And they want and often expect others to just grab it. Yet sometimes it takes weeks and months, and even years, for that to happen—*unless* they have documented standards and have taken the time to say, "If you're going to play on my team, here are the standards we live by."

**SUPER PERFORMERS ACTUALLY HAVE THEIR WRITTEN STANDARDS BECOME PART OF THEIR CULTURE.**

The super performers actually have these written guidelines or standards become part of their culture. They've taken the time to document their standards, post them, and teach them, so when new people are added it's an easy matter of saying, "Here are our standards." Their new people are not left to wonder for weeks or months how things work or what's important. They are shown the standards right up front so they can produce at a higher level, and everyone wins.

I'm convinced that standards go way beyond just adding someone effectively to your team. I believe standards are a big part of the mastery level. People at that level have standards for themselves, and they have standards for others that either deploy on their behalf, join their team, or both.

**Personal standards**. Personal standards set the stage for minimal distractions, guide your decisions, and help you say "no" more often so you can get rid of *Low-Leverage Activities*. Do you want to live in mastery? If so, make sure you've thought through all these pieces.

Let me share with you my twelve personal standards—twelve specific things I do every day:

1. Each morning pray for wisdom. I start each morning in prayer. I pray for wisdom every day. If I'm in the shower, I'm praying. While I'm shaving, I'm praying about the day.

2. Do team huddles or stimulate huddles for my team. Each morning I line up my team, either by phone, e-mail, or in person, and we

huddle about all the things we need to do that day. Are you doing that with your team? Even if I'm traveling, I'll send a note by e-mail and my team will huddle without me, using the e-mail I sent. I believe incredible synergy comes from doing team huddles, and many leaders miss that.

3. Glance at my new business opportunities to keep them fresh in my mind. My relationship manager sends me an e-mail every morning, and I look at it and think about the opportunities that are ahead of me. I want to keep those fresh in my mind every day so I have it down tight.

4. Determine my top priorities for the day or the week. We have a master to-do list that we look at every day and determine the top priorities. I look at the master list to see what my personal priorities are, because throughout the day I want to make sure I'm doing the things that are at the top of my list. How about you? Do you get down in the weeds too much, or do you lift up and really zoom in on your priorities? Remember what I said earlier: It's not about activity; it's about productivity. At the end of the day I want to know that I got the most important things done—not that I just got a ton of things done.

5. Touch my family and my team members inspirationally in some way. That means I have to smile. I have to get up in the morning and love my wife by sending her a note or smiling and saying nice things to her when she walks into the kitchen. If my kids are home, that means I'm loving them. If we're on a vacation, I'm loving them. When I walk up the stairs to my studio I want to have a smile on my face and be inspirational to my team. How about you? Are you committed to being the type of leader who impacts your family members and anybody you touch each day?

6. Compliment and communicate appreciation for those around me. I am convinced that many people miss this one. When is the last time you heard someone say, "Would you quit appreciating me?" Probably never, because everyone wants to be appreciated, right? How about you? When you get a nice note or an e-mail, when someone says nice things to you, or when you get a thank you, don't you think about

it over and over? People crave appreciation.

7. Stretch, flex, and breathe with both confidence and gratitude. I want to keep my body healthy, and I want to appreciate everything I have. Gratitude makes me a better person. There are all kinds of opportunities to dwell on the negative things that happen. I got my phone wet a few weeks ago, and of course it quit working. Was that a problem? Yes. However, I chose not to dwell on that, and instead to be grateful for all my blessings. That's what I want to do every day.

8. Organize and rationalize to keep things clean. (Be a river, not a reservoir.) If you were to look at my closets, you would see that they're clean. And the same with my car. I'm constantly giving things away to get them out of my life and keep things clean and organized.

How about you? Do you have things in your closet that you will never wear again, and they just keep stacking up? If you're not going to wear it, get rid of it. What about your desk? Clutter sucks your energy, and keeping things organized and tight frees your mind and energy for bigger and better things.

9. Visualize my own goals (short- and long-term) with focus and clarity. What you have real clarity about and focus on is what you execute. I visualize everything, and I study my vision board every day. For most of my girls' lives, I visualized who they were going to marry. As a matter of fact, when they were three and six years old we got a wedding picture frame, and we put a picture of them on the bride side. On the groom side we put a list of twelve characteristics of the guys they would eventually date and marry. Over the years, we talked about it and prayed about it, and they became the young ladies who would attract guys with those twelve characteristics. And now I have a son-in-law who matches that list.

> VISUALIZE YOUR GOALS WITH FOCUS AND CLARITY. WHAT YOU HAVE REAL CLARITY ABOUT AND FOCUS ON IS WHAT YOU EXECUTE.

How about you? Are you visualizing with your kids who they're going to become and who they're going to marry?

How about on the health side? If you open my medicine cabinet, you'll see visualizations of the type of body I want to have. I look at it every day, and it motivates me. I encourage you to do exactly the same.

10. Model exceptional behavior, including enjoying life. How many people fill their lives with all kinds of cool things and then don't enjoy life? I encourage you to stop and enjoy the moment. If you have sunshine, enjoy the sunshine. If you have rain, find ways to enjoy the rain. I know people who have swimming pools, and after the first three or four years they use them maybe three times a year. I enjoy my pool every day I can. I swim sixty, seventy, or eighty days out of the year. I want to love and enjoy every single day of my life. How about you?

11. Eat healthy food. I have my team make sure nothing gets in front of me that's not healthy, because I get tempted just like everyone else does. I don't want unhealthy food in my pantries or refrigerators. I want every food I see to be healthy. In the last section of this chapter, I'll be talking about habits, and one of my strategic six is the habit of staying healthy. It's right up there among the six habits I think will contribute the most to your success.

12. Doing favors for those who are a part of my life. I make giving gifts an important part of my life. In fact, last Christmas I gave away 860 gifts. I handwrite notes and send them to hundreds of people a year; I e-mail out best ideas to people; and when I find videos I think are valuable, I send the links to people. I'm constantly doing favors for others so I can help them be their best. How about you? Do you make doing favors for others a standard in your life?

There you have my twelve personal daily standards that help me live a life of mastery. I hope I've helped you think about the standards that should be on your list; perhaps you could even use some of mine.

**Professional standards**. These could be just for you and those you might delegate to, or they could be for those you recruit to your team or organization. They could be for your department if you happen to run one, or they could be for a whole enterprise or even multiple companies in your holding company if you happen to be at that level. When I work with executives, I push them to get clear on their professional standards.

Let me share a story about one of my clients. He's among the richest 400 in the world. In fact, last year I believe he was the 172nd richest guy in the world. He's worth about $8 billion. He has forty-two companies, and he brings the presidents of all of his companies together once a year for what he calls a "pride meeting." And do you know what he does during these pride meetings? He has all forty-two of his presidents go over his standards and tell how their companies are living up to them. The way he builds this meeting is quite impressive, and it's even more impressive that all forty-two companies are living his standards. The man is special!

I really admire people who move to the top like that, and I want to help you do the same thing. So I'm going to share my professional standards with you so you can get an understanding of what a really *High-Performing Team* with outstanding performance standards can look like. I've modified them just a little to make it easier for you to model any you see that you want to utilize. I have mine posted in every room in my office, and I encourage you to do the same. I also have my team include them in the very first in-person interview when they're recruiting someone for our firm. In fact, that's one of our standards. They tell the person being interviewed that if we make them an offer, they need to know that these standards are solid expectations of how we operate, and they need to make sure they can live with them.

1. Continuous learning. When someone comes to work for me, they will be promoted and rewarded for constantly learning.

2. Accountability. Everyone in my organization must maintain personal and organizational commitment to continuous accountability in objectively measurable ways. For example, since making lists is one of our standards, they have to make lists, and their effectiveness is measured against their completed lists.

3. Simplicity. Make complex things simple. I don't like complex things. Narrow it down so everyone can understand it, and then get it done.

4. HLAs. Know your HLAs and live by them so you reduce LLAs.

5. Over-communicate and calculate. This helps to ensure everyone's efforts are maximized. As I said earlier, it's okay if we send two e-mails about the same thing. I don't want things falling through the cracks.

6. Start with the end in mind. What do we want to accomplish? Whether it's an e-mail, a project, or a book, we want to make sure we have the end in mind and the objective(s) we want to accomplish.

7. Everything organized all the time. That's *all* the time. It's not five or six days a week; it's seven days a week. It's not when we feel like it; it's all the time.

8. Make and utilize lists. Ask my team; they'll tell you we're into lists.

9. Respect, reward, and appreciate team members. We want to make sure everyone lives out the whole idea of respect and appreciation.

10. Team support. We want overlap, and we want to have people covering for each other.

At the very foundation of all of my standards, both personal and professional, is my mantra: give value and do more than is expected. It overarches everything I do personally and all that both my team and I do professionally. You might consider adopting that as a standard for yourself.

There are my big ten, with a bonus foundational standard. I hope you see some you can use. I want you to really get the fact that you need to have both personal and professional standards, and you need to own them.

Before we go on to the next section, let me share one more story.

Would you like to know where I got this whole conviction about standards and living in mastery? It came from a project I did about twenty years ago, when I was helping turn Chrysler around. In 1991, Lee Iacocca was going out, and Chrysler was on its last leg. I got called in on a small assignment, and I vowed to be one of the number one guys in this special group selected to help Chrysler. We set a vision to become one of the best companies in the world. Five-and-a-half years later, Chrysler was featured on the front of *Forbes* magazine as one of the most admired companies in America. And this is what we did to accomplish that amazing feat: We developed a set of performance standards, which we took to the 110,000 employees Chrysler had at the time, through about 4,000 dealerships in about 80 countries, and we had each dealership commit to living up to those standards. That experience gave me a clear understanding of what can

WE DEVELOPED A SET OF PERFORMANCE STANDARDS, WHICH WE TOOK TO 110,000 EMPLOYEES CHRYSLER HAD AT THE TIME, THROUGH ABOUT 4,000 DEALERSHIPS IN ABOUT 80 COUNTRIES, AND WE HAD EACH DEALERSHIP COMMIT TO LIVING UP TO THOSE STANDARDS. FIVE-AND-A-HALF YEARS LATER, CHRYSLER WAS FEATURED ON THE FRONT OF FORBES MAGAZINE AS ONE OF THE MOST ADMIRED COMPANIES IN AMERICA.

happen if we set powerful standards, make them clear, and cascade them down through the entire organization.

And I know you want that kind of success for yourself, as well. So let me end this section with one of my quotes: "Business is like a game of chess. To achieve mastery you have to make the right strategic moves." Having documented standards is one of them.

# LIFE TEAM

Now we're going to talk about another concept I developed—having an exceptional *Life Team* around you to help you live in mastery. I believe you're going to love this concept, because most of the top achievers I work with do. In reality, you probably already have a partial *Life Team* around you, and you just don't know it yet, at least by this term. In this section, though, we're going to take it to another whole level.

We talked about building *High-Performing Teams* earlier. Now we're going to talk about *Life Teams*, which is a similar yet different concept. I'm talking about surrounding yourself with *Life Team* members who have gifts and talents that complement your own

> SURROUND YOURSELF WITH *LIFE TEAM* MEMBERS WHO HAVE GIFTS AND TALENTS THAT COMPLEMENT YOUR OWN AND HELP YOU DO LIFE WELL.

and who give you insights and advice and help you execute. In short, they help you do life well.

For example, people often ask me how I have the time to author forty-five books. Well, the behind-the-scenes deal is that I have a super-strong *Life Team*. Some people on my team have been helping me with researching, writing, editing, and proofing for two decades. They know me, they know my content, they know my thinking, they know my processes, and they know my style. It's important to have *Life Team* members you trust and who connect with you.

You may be thinking, "Yes, it's a wonderful concept, Tony. And you can do it because you have all kinds of money and you can make it happen. Yet how about me? Can just anyone do this?" Yes, you can. Be open-minded to what I'm saying here, and I think you'll be pleasantly surprised.

**Life team members are handpicked. They're smart people. Sometimes they're in groups, and sometimes they're individuals, and they all have specific areas of expertise that can be leveraged on your behalf.** They can range from advisors to your air-conditioner man. They can include your dentist, your doctor, and even your jeweler. You see, one of the absolute best ways to get things done and really execute is through other people. And having people in your life who you know and trust and who know and trust you can create a winning situation. Among other things, you avoid wasted time looking for someone who truly has that expertise.

> LIFE TEAM MEMBERS ARE HANDPICKED. THEY'RE SMART PEOPLE. SOMETIMES THEY'RE IN GROUPS, AND SOMETIMES THEY'RE INDIVIDUALS, AND THEY ALL HAVE SPECIFIC AREAS OF EXPERTISE THAT CAN BE LEVERAGED ON YOUR BEHALF.

Let's talk about your air-conditioner guy for a minute. Say your air conditioner in your home goes out. What happens if you don't have a trusted air conditioner man like I do? (His name is Calvin.) You end up going on Google and looking through the list of air-conditioning companies, or you might call someone to get a referral. You're experiencing stress because your air conditioner's out, and you have to find someone you hope you can trust who can come out and fix it. If you already had an air-conditioner guy on your *Life Team*, you could just call him—someone you already know you can trust and who knows your home—to come over and fix it. I recommend that you have a person on your team for every segment of your life, and I'm going to talk about the different segments of a *Life Team* in just a moment.

The right relationships allow you to call upon your *Life Team* members at any time. Once or twice a month on a Sunday afternoon I go over to my friend Jay's barn (his office that was built to look like a barn), and he mentors me. And sometimes when I go, his attorney is there as well. David Hammer, who is also my attorney, is a very special and talented man—a valuable *Life Team* member—and on a Sunday afternoon he and Jay often go over the deals he's handling for Jay. Now think about this. Have you ever been so connected with an attorney that you can call him or her to come over on a Sunday afternoon? I can text my CPA just about any time and can get a question answered if I need to make a big purchase or I need to make a decision that relates to my taxes. In fact, one of my very best friends is also my family attorney and is a *Life Team* member who helps me oversee all portions of my life.

The right team members will be those you have sought out and tested. And once you find them, they need to be loved on and appreciated. For example, my pool guy had been with me for six or eight years, constantly taking outstanding care of the pool in my back yard. For his anniversary, I sent him a gift certificate so he could take his wife to the Ritz Carlton and have dinner on me. He was blown away. My thinking was, *Here's a guy who, for six or eight years, has taken care of my pool, and I never have to worry about it.* He deserved my appreciation.

> THE RIGHT TEAM MEMBERS WILL BE THOSE YOU HAVE SOUGHT OUT AND TESTED. AND ONCE YOU FIND THEM, THEY NEED TO BE LOVED AND APPRECIATED.

Now let's go into the details of how to build and shape your own *Life Team*. First, I want you to get the mindset of the value of having a *Life Team* firmly implanted in your mind. Got it? Okay, I'm going to walk you through it step by step.

You have to intentionally place people onto your *Life Team*. These will be trusted, talented individuals you place around you, who can either advise you or actually do things for you to help you execute. Let's go through my system, and I'll tell you specifically about my *Life Team*, which will stimulate your thinking about yours.

The first segment of your *Life Team* is your home team. Do you have someone who mows your yard, or maybe a landscaper? I have a landscaper who is also a horticulturist, so when I need something done on my trees (I have 120 on my estate), I can call him, and he can tell me the distinctions I need. I also have an electrician, and I have a plumber. Here's the kind of relationship I have with my plumber: Sometimes I'll call, and instead of his coming out and charging me, he'll say, "Just do this and you can probably fix it." He tells me to do something that's really quick and simple, and it works, and all of a sudden I've saved a service call. When you have that kind of relationship with people on your home team, you can really make things happen. At Christmas time my assistants make a phone call to Mia, and Mia comes out and puts the Christmas lights up, and then she comes out and takes them down after Christmas (and I don't even have to call her). It's so convenient to be able to tap into people who can make things happen for you on your home *Life Team*.

On the professional side, I have my attorney. Actually, I have several different attorneys for different needs in my life. I have a trust attorney, a deal attorney (David), and a general attorney, who has been my attorney for thirty years. I have my CPA. And I have my pilots—my small plane pilot, my big plane pilot, and my helicopter pilot. I have my banker, who is also my friend and is one of my *Life Team* members I can call on any time. In fact, I have two good bankers. If you don't have a good banker, you should find one. And I have several writers. Nonie has been writing for me for almost twenty years. Think about the value of having someone write for you who really knows who you are. And I have a graphic artist; my daughter does most of that for me.

Now let's go on to the personal segment. You probably have a stylist who cuts your hair. Are you loving on the person who takes care of your hair for you? And maybe you have a jeweler. I have a personal coach, Mark Pantak, who has been with me for thirty years. I have two drivers; I so appreciate them and they truly support me. Think about all the different people who take care of you. I even have a guy who works in the Apple store that I can call if something goes wrong with my iPhone. Think of all the stores you shop in on a regular basis. Is there someone who has waited on you and taken care of you for a long time? Or maybe you have someone inside a restaurant that you can call and get in when no one else can.

I also have my health *Life Team* members. I have different trainers who help me every week, and I have different doctors who help me. Dr. Light is my primary doctor, and he helps me really live at peak performance.

And I have spiritual mentors I consider part of my *Life Team*, like my pastor, my father-in-law, Steve Dulin, and Dr. Robert Rohm. Then I have my business mentors: Jay Rodgers, Scott Bennett, Buz Barlow, Frank Holly, and Don Baker, who pour into my life from a business standpoint.

> Now, one more thing to help you really own this: You may be thinking, *I don't want to spend the money.* I encourage you not to go there. Let me share with you a powerful book that sparked my thinking to a whole new level about two decades ago. It's called *Your Money or Your Life.* It provides a formula to help you calculate how much of your life you trade for whatever you're spending money on. You take the money you earn on a nonpassive basis and divide that by the number of hours you dedicate to your work, so you can be really clear on how much money you actually make for any given hour or minute. Then you can understand how many hours of your life it takes to pay for whatever you're buying or spending money on, and you can make a wise and informed choice about whether that product or activity is worth the cost of the hours of life energy you would need to spend. It's really a powerful tool that helped me understand that I had been doing that for years—building a *Life Team* around me to do the things I was not good at or didn't like to do, or that I didn't need a particular expertise in, because my life energy was better invested doing the things I enjoy and that I excel in.

Sometimes your *Life Team* members will give you insight you wouldn't have gained otherwise. Sometimes they do things for you so you can execute better or faster. Sometimes you have them do something because you don't like doing it or because you don't have the expertise. When you calculate the investment, I think you'll find that having *Life Team* members takes you down a wise path.

As you assemble your *Life Team*, make sure you have a very organized list of the members on your phone and on your computer. I even have a template for it that you can request by e-mailing me at info@tonyjeary.com. Evaluate your *Life Team* members regularly, and shift or update your players as needed. For example when your kids grow up, you no longer need a child-care team member. Maybe you find that you need multiple attorneys or an additional banker.

Here are my four tips for building and maintaining a *Life Team*:

> BE A PERSON WHO CAN REALLY MOVE MOUNTAINS BECAUSE YOU HAVE BUILT, ASSEMBLED, APPRECIATED, AND NOURISHED A POWERFUL TEAM OF PEOPLE AROUND YOU.

1. Really grasp the concept of a *Life Team* and see who else could be added to your team to help you reach your goals.

2. Note each on your phone, indicating their role along with their name and info.

3. Build the list through referrals, and upgrade as needed.

4. Make sure you respect, support, and really appreciate each *Life Team* member on your list.

Be a person who can really move mountains because you have built, assembled, appreciated, and nourished a powerful team of people around you.

# HABITS

About sixteen years ago, profound influence came into my life from reading the book *7 Habits of Highly Effective People* by Stephen Covey. Perhaps that book has impacted you, as well. Habits are powerful, and they're a huge part of the mastery puzzle. I've been studying habits for years, and now I'm going to give you my best research, which has helped me and others really win in this area. Developing good habits allows you to master the things in life that are important to you and helps you weed out bad habits. The bottom line is, good habits make you more productive and set you up to better succeed.

**THE RESULTS WE GET IN OUR LIVES CAN BE DIRECTLY ATTRIBUTED TO THE HABITS WE FORM.**

Aristotle once said, **"We are what we repeatedly do. Excellence, then, is not an act, but a habit."** If he's right, and I believe he is, then the results we get in our lives can be directly attributed to the habits we form.

Sometimes you see an individual from afar demonstrate a level of mastery so specialized and so magnificent that it's easy to think that person is just gifted. And, yes, I believe God has given all of us certain gifts. I also believe that, gifted or not, if you want more of the title of this book, more of the right RESULTS Faster—taking your vision to reality in compressed time frames—then you must get your habits right.

For decades I've worked with and advised the best masters across industries all over the world, and I've come to believe that there are three basic steps to becoming a master at anything, to live at the mastery level in your parenting, marriage, leadership, mentoring, health, or any other facet of your life:

**Step one:** You have to be aware of the different levels (good, great and mastery) and know in what level you are operating.

**Step two:** You must understand the benefits of living at the mastery level so your "want-to factor" kicks into high gear. Then you are self-inspired and motivated because you truly understand the feelings you can experience by living at this success level.

**Step three:** You must execute to the point of habit, where the right things (in both thinking and doing) become automatic. Your habits allow you to produce incredible results over and over.

Any of us can achieve mastery in any area of our lives if we're truly willing to commit our habits to it entirely. And that includes habitually raising our (clearly documented) standards and not tolerating anything less than the very best. This is what it takes to be a true master.

We're going to cover four things in this section: the concept of automatic, my strategic six habits, connecting with your values, and developing excellent habits that really support your overall success.

## THE CONCEPT OF AUTOMATIC

Let me give you a personal example that explains this concept. At the beginning of each year I look at and set up the new year by saying, *What do I want to accomplish this year?* And the number one item on my list this year is to become automatic. I want to take everything to another whole level of automatic. Let me explain how that applies to you.

I believe that mastery comes with the freedom to have built-in *margin time* so you can put your efforts and energies where you want them. If you want to live in mastery, then you have to be strategic and intentional about moving things into the automatic zone—and that, of course, involves habits.

> IF YOU WANT TO LIVE IN MASTERY, THEN YOU HAVE TO BE STRATEGIC AND INTENTIONAL ABOUT MOVING THINGS INTO THE AUTOMATIC ZONE—AND THAT, OF COURSE, INVOLVES HABITS.

I believe you can get more automatic by setting systems in place for things other people do for you and allowing technology to take over some of the tactical things in your life—even by using something as simple as a sprinkler system. One day I realized that my sprinkler system could be expanded to automate another task besides keeping my lawn, trees, and shrubs watered. I added a zone to fill my pool, so the pool now gets filled automatically every day. Making tasks happen automatically frees you up for other, more important things. When I get a long-term prescription, I have it mailed to me monthly, and I do the same with my supplements. I put everything I can on automatic. I'm blessed with a home team that handles my clothes. I even have an automatic system for dry cleaning; when I set my clothes out, they go out to the cleaners. When they come back, I have people who put them in my closet and keep it organized. I automate everything I can with habits, and I want you to think about that as well.

The real impact comes when you automate not only the tasks that others and technology can do for you, but also the foundational things you do for yourself that can accelerate your success. Habits are a way of putting yourself on autopilot or automatic, and yet they are so much more. They can be directed ahead of time so the end result is what you really want.

> YOU HAVE TO STRATEGICALLY LIFT UP AND SEE THE BIG PICTURE, AND THEN MAKE WHATEVER CHANGES ARE NECESSARY TO IMPROVE YOUR HABITS.

Remember, the results we get in life can be directly attributed to the habits we form. We continue in our habits because we crave and reward the outcomes. Think about it. How often do you keep a bad habit because you crave what it gives you?

Here's a profound truth: You have to strategically lift up and see the big picture, and then make whatever changes are necessary to improve your habits. If you're intentional about developing good habits, you will eventually replace the bad habits. It's like growing grass. If you grow grass, it chokes out the weeds. If you put good habits in, you can choke out your bad habits. Getting rid of bad habits by bringing in more good habits is a big piece of the mastery puzzle.

Research shows that 40 percent of our lives are made up of habitual activities. I would like to keep mine at 60, 70, or even 80 percent. People who live in mastery have developed habits that automate many things in their lives. For example, working out is a positive habit that supports our success. Endorphins are released, which give you energy and make you happy, and there's an added mental reward of accomplishment. When working out becomes an automatic habit for you, it becomes as natural to your life as breathing.

In my own life, I deploy six strategic foundational habits. And I teach these same powerful habits to my high achieving clients because I know they can help them live in that mastery level. I want to share these strategic six with you right now:

1. **Strategic List Making and List Managing.** I'm not talking about just daily to-dos; I'm talking about putting every single thing you do into a list format—your HLAs, your goals, your spouse's goals, your kids' goals, your POIs, your *Life Team*, and so on. So many people think, *I can remember this,* so they don't write it down. That just fills up and chokes your mind. You can release things from your mind when you put them down in a list, because you know you can go back and look at them later.

If you form the habit of looking at your to-do list ten, twelve, and fourteen times a day, then you don't get to the end of the day and think, *How did I do?* Throughout the day you see that you're accomplishing the things you should. In fact, it's a good idea to strategically look at your list sometime during mid-afternoon each day and ask, *How many of my priorities have I accomplished, and what do I have left?* Then you can take the last few hours of your day and really get going to make sure you end the day with the most important things completed.

2. **Strategic Goal Setting**. I believe you've seen by my enthusiasm throughout this book that I am passionate about goal setting, and I hope I've made the point by now that you have to be strategic about it. In fact, if you want to live in mastery, it's crucial that you make goal setting one of your strategic habits—something you do habitually every week or every quarter or every year. If you establish it as a strategic habit, then you'll do it whether you feel inspired to or not. When you have an effective goal-setting system, you can look at it every few days and see how you're progressing and then adjust it accordingly.

3. **Strategic Health.** We can have everything in the world, and yet if

we don't have our health, does it really matter? There are two specific elements involved here:

a. Exercise habits

b. The right eating habits

If you don't exercise, you won't have a healthy body. If you don't eat right, you won't have a healthy body. You need to examine every bite you put in your body, even down to the point of being strategic about your snacking. Set up the habits that will help you be the healthiest.

4. **Strategic Learning.** Are you habitual about putting things into your life that will help you learn? For example, when you subscribe to magazines or blogs that support your goals, you're putting things on automatic mode that will help you habitually learn. Almost every night, I read and watch videos that will help me learn. I often go to bed watching bios, because I like to hear about other people's success stories and learn their distinctions. And lately I've taken my strategic learning up a notch. When I hear distinctions that apply to me as I'm listening to those bios, I list those distinctions in my phone.

I'm so into strategically managing my habits that I've figured out how to combine two of them into an *Elegant Solution.* I've put a flip-chart in my gym, and I've asked my trainers, while they're setting up for me in the mornings, to write out things on the flipchart I can be learning. Then between sets I go over and learn. Strategic learning, strategic health.

5. **Strategic Altruism.** That's being automatic about constantly encouraging, supporting, helping, and doing things for others. Novelist and philosopher Ayn Rand once said, "A creative man is motivated by the desire to achieve, not by the desire to beat others." As you go through life, do you have a habit of helping other people?

6. **Strategic Willpower.** Willpower is like a muscle. It can grow big, and it can get tired. With the right management it can be strengthened to positively impact your decisions, like the decision to eat correctly. Develop the habit of eating every two hours so you don't let yourself get super hungry, because if you do you gorge and then overeat until you feel stuffed. We've all been there, and we all know what it's like

not to have that discipline. Establishing the habit of willpower and managing it is an important piece.

How are you doing on these six strategic habits? Did you find there's room for improvement? All six are crucial to your success

I firmly believe that if we align our habits with our values, we will have a much more congruent and masterful life. I want to walk you through an exercise that I believe will help you really grab hold of this concept. Think back to Chapter 2 when we were talking about values, and I asked you to identify your top ten. Pull out that list of your top ten values right now, and we're going to connect habits to each one of them. I'm going to share mine with you so you can really grasp what I'm talking about and model this exercise for yourself.

> **IF WE ALIGN OUR HABITS WITH OUR VALUES, WE WILL HAVE A MUCH MORE CONGRUENT AND MASTERFUL LIFE.**

1. My number one value is **inner peace**. So what habits have I set up that support having inner peace? The first one is gratitude. I count my blessings each morning, and I balance contentment and enjoying what I have with constantly looking at my goals and aspirations and seeing where I want to go. And the second habit that supports my inner peace is breathing and reflecting. I often do that in my outdoor results lounge behind my studio. If inner peace is one of your values, you might consider gratitude and breathing and reflecting.

2. My second value is **personal faith**. One of my habits, then, is to constantly pray throughout the day.

3. Number three is **recognition**. I love compliments and I love to give compliments, so I'm constantly looking for ways I can encourage others. And I have another habit of intentionally looking at people's achievements so I can acknowledge and recognize them.

4. My fourth value is **altruism**. One of my ongoing habits is to look for ways to be of value to others, and I have strategically built my arsenal that helps me do that.

5. My next value is **productivity**, one of my favorites. This is where I apply my habit of making and managing lists. I work my lists diligently, and I encourage my team to do the same. I drive for completion. Partial execution doesn't count for me. I want things done.

6. Good **health** is my next value. I apply my strategic health habit by training daily and eating healthy (approximately every ninety minutes). I'm strategic about my snacking. Another habit is to go to bed early and sleep eight hours a night. All of these are habits that lead to my good health.

7. My **family** is obviously one of my top values, and here's a habit that supports that: I often schedule activities of interest, fun, and learning with my family members. Another is that I carefully ask questions and listen to my kids. My daughter often says to me, "Dad, I love it that you listen to me." If you're around your kids and you're not listening, maybe that's a habit you need to pick up. Another habit is that I give sincere compliments to my kids, encouraging them and building up their self-esteem. Perhaps that's something you should do, as well.

8. My next value is **lifestyle**. I make it a habit to enjoy my life every day. Every day is like a weekend to me. And I'm learning to set more and more things up into the automatic so I can maximize my time even more and enjoy my lifestyle.

9. Another one of my top ten values is **organization**. My habit is to keep everything organized all the time, and my team members help me as well. That includes my vehicles, my home, my office, my studio, my backpack, and even my health closet. I make labels and lists and checklists on an ongoing basis to support always being organized.

10. My final top value is **wisdom**. Since one of my strategic six hab-

its is learning, that means I'm always reading excellent books, listening to outstanding CDs, or studying materials that support my goals. Wisdom is my business. As a coach, I need to really be on top of my game, so I have a habit of continually having new insights coming into my life.

Now, using my top values and habits as a model, you can go through the same exercise and identify the habits that will support your top ten values.

As an added bonus on the subject of habits, let me share a little of my personal story on health. (As a side note, I teamed up with a couple of doctors a few years ago and wrote a book called *Ultimate Health*, because I wanted to prove that you really could reverse your age if you had the right habits.)

You may remember my story about having breakfast with my client Ron, and I could tell he had lost quite a bit of weight since I'd seen him last. He's the one that busted my belief about orange juice being healthy. That's when I realized that I had no clue about how the body works. A week later, I went to my wife's grandmother's funeral. My sister-in-law was there, and she, too, had lost quite a bit of weight. I said, "You look terrific! What are you doing?" She said, "I'm counting calories."

Now, understand that I had worked out for years, and yet I was still a bit on the heavy side. I decided right then and there that I needed to make a change. Those two encounters made such an impact on me that I established a new habit right away of learning how the body works. And I went from 25 percent body fat down to 10 percent, and from weighing over 200 pounds down to 170 pounds. I went from a 38-inch waist down to a 31-inch waist. I got really serious about living healthy, and I'd like to help you do the same.

Once I had the awareness, I knew I had to change my habits. I'd like to share with you the six new personal habits I established to support my success in the area of health.

1. **Eating well**. It really is what you eat. Actually, it's what you absorb, although eating well is a big part of it, and that includes

strategic snacking.

2. **Exercise**. There are four pieces of the exercise puzzle: stretching, balancing, cardio, and weight resistance. You need to include all four of those in your exercise bucket.

3. **Managing stress**. You have to use self-talk here and be able to ask yourself, Does it really matter? It was a habit I had to get into.

4. **Rest**. I used to brag and say, "I can get by on four, five, or six hours' sleep, because I'm so disciplined." What I didn't realize, though, is what that was doing with the hormones in my body. Studies show that sleeping seven or eight hours a night is best.

5. **Relaxing**. It's so important to get into the habit of relaxing and enjoying your life.

6. **Breathing well**. This involves stepping back, changing or finding the right environment, then breathing and thinking about your future, your blessings, and the big picture of life.

All six of those habits are important pieces to the health puzzle. Successful people are attracted to healthy people. Think about that. People want to be around other people who are healthy.

Habits, both good and bad, need to be strategically managed for anyone desiring to operate in the mastery level. I encourage you to put as many things as you can on automatic and incorporate whatever good habits you need to help you move to that level. Maybe that includes adopting my strategic six habits. Make sure you connect your values to your habits so you'll have a much more congruent and masterful life. And finally, establish habits that will lead you to live a healthy life.

I said something in casual conversation with a friend recently, and I want to share with you part of my friend's e-mail to me the next day:

> You made a comment yesterday during our phone conversation. You said something to the effect of "Three years ago I woke up and asked myself one of my favorite questions—MOLO— *What do I want more of in my life?*" And you answered yourself

with, *I want more of the same things; I have what I want in my life—I want more of the same things.* You mentioned your yard, your cars, your wife and your children. Life is what you want it to be.

It occurred to me that you are getting exactly what you want in life; and stated another way, in reference to a quote by Arthur W. Jones, you are "perfectly aligned to get the results you are getting." And this is working for you.

I share this with you because I want you to see that our habits can produce such an incredible life that our response can truly be, "Just more of the same," when someone asks what we want more of. As we move to the close of this book I hope you are persuaded that you can indeed get the results you want in life when you align powerful habits with Clarity, Focus, and Execution, and all the other distinctions I've shared in this, my life's work.

## Results Audit

Remember the Results Audit you took when you first started this book? Now that you've read through the entire book and hopefully absorbed many of the ideas and principles I've given you that will help you move your vision to reality, assess yourself again and see how far you've progressed.

Again, go through all seven areas—Strategic Mindset, Clarity, Focus, Execution, Force Multipliers, Leadership, and Mastery—and rate yourself between one and five on each one to see where you are now. My guess is that your numbers have been pushed up significantly since you started.

# The Results Audit: After

*What gets measured, gets improved.*
—Peter Drucker

Please take a few moments and rate yourself on this simple self-audit of where you currently operate in each of the seven primary areas covered in this course. 1 is low, 5 is high. Check the level you think best represents your current level of mastery in each area now that you have read and absorbed the contents of this book. If you still have areas you want to improve to get the results you want, go back and study and apply the principles I set out in those areas. Better yet, enroll in the *RESULTS Faster!* online course or make an appointment to meet with me in my private studio.

| Module 1 | Level 1 | Level 2 | Level 3 | Level 4 | Level 5 |
|---|---|---|---|---|---|
| **Strategic Thinking:** *How intentional am I at managing my thinking?* <br><br> **My Rating:** | I don't know how to manage my thinking or what my beliefs are. I focus mostly on activities, and I'm very busy all the time. | I realize that my thoughts can affect my productivity, and beliefs influence my actions. I'd like to be more strategic in what I do. | I practice thinking strategically, and I have identified many of my good and bad beliefs. I assess my day based on what I believe will produce the best results. | My thoughts are mostly directive and purposeful. I actively work to eliminate false beliefs while strengthening beliefs that keep me focused. My days are focused and productive. | I use my thoughts strategically to guide me toward my goals. I live an authentic life based on my chosen beliefs. I consistently ask, "What's the best use of my time right now?" |

| Module 2 | Level 1 | Level 2 | Level 3 | Level 4 | Level 5 |
|---|---|---|---|---|---|
| **Clarity:** *How clear am I about what's important in my life and work?* <br><br> **My Rating:** | I have very little idea about my life's purpose, passions, what makes me happy, or my values or goals. | I believe in having a clear picture of what's important in life, including my passion, purpose, and what makes me happy. I think about my values and have one or two clear goals. | I know what's important to me in life, including my values and goals. I'm putting some of my values into practice, and I am implementing written action plans for my goals. | I am motivated by my list of purpose, passion, values, and goals, and I am following a clear plan to create a life designed around what's most important to me. | My purpose, passion, values, and goals guide my daily decisions and actions. I am absolutely clear on the results I will achieve and how I choose to live. |

| Module 3 | Level 1 | Level 2 | Level 3 | Level 4 | Level 5 |
|---|---|---|---|---|---|
| **Focus:** *How focused am I in my life and work?* <br><br> **My Rating:** | I find myself easily distracted and/or bogged down in insignificant, time-consuming tasks. I say "yes" too often to other people's priorities. | I am working to improve my focusing skills. I know what I need to do more of and less of to be more productive, and I'm figuring out my High-Leverage Activities (HLAs). I try to say "yes" only to what matters most. | I prioritize the things I need to do more of and delegate what I can. I focus on activities that will produce the greatest results and usually have the courage to say "no" to other priorities. | Each day I focus on things that are relevant to my strategic agenda, success, and achievement. I accomplish my daily HLAs 80% of the time and say "no" to anything that does not match these activities. | I concentrate solely on completing strategic goals and objectives. I am more productive than ever and deliver outstanding results on time or early. |

| Module 4 | Level 1 | Level 2 | Level 3 | Level 4 | Level 5 |
|---|---|---|---|---|---|
| **Execution:** *How well do I manage my time and effort to get things done?* **My Rating:** | I procrastinate and have trouble delivering results on time and fail to ask others for help because I am not a good communicator. | I am somewhat better at getting things done on time. I occasionally call in more resources to help, but I need to get better at enrolling others. | I schedule my time effectively, and ask for help/additional resources early. I am comfortable in sharing my ideas and viewpoints with others and understanding their needs. | I execute my plans and deliver results on time. I am good at recruiting and encouraging others, giving value, and helping them get what they want as they help me get what I want. | I am exceptional in exceeding expectations and delivering results on time or early. I communicate brilliantly with others, and I move them to take action so we all produce results faster. |

| Module 5 | Level 1 | Level 2 | Level 3 | Level 4 | Level 5 |
|---|---|---|---|---|---|
| **Force Multipliers:** *How well do I use leverage to get things done faster and more efficiently?* **My Rating:** | I tend to do everything myself, and I have trouble getting things done. My preparation is poor. | I use some tools to help me out, and I'm getting better at preparing and reaching out to others for help. I spend time in advance to get ready for big projects or events. | I often use tools, preparation, and my network to help me achieve results faster. | I seek out and use the best tools, people, and strategies to help leverage my own efforts. I prepare relentlessly for any opportunity I'm presented with. | I leverage my efforts in multiple ways and through my extensive network of connections. Preparation is part of my daily practice, and my results are spectacular. |

| Module 6 | Level 1 | Level 2 | Level 3 | Level 4 | Level 5 |
|---|---|---|---|---|---|
| **Leadership:** *How well do I nourish and foster the environments that support extraordinary decision making?* <br><br> **My Rating:** | I may have a vision, but I don't communicate it well. People have little confidence in my leadership because they don't really know who I am. | I have articulated a vision to my team, and they understand what we want to achieve. I am clear about my strengths, and I want to help my team develop theirs. | The team is inspired by the goals and vision I communicate to them. I discover what my team wants and then encourage their efforts to succeed. | The team is self-directed and focused, and my job as leader is simply to empower them to excel. We are achieving great things together. | The team has produced outstanding results, and they attribute much of our success to my support and leadership. |

| Module 7 | Level 1 | Level 2 | Level 3 | Level 4 | Level 5 |
|---|---|---|---|---|---|
| **Mastery:** *How committed am I to consistently produce extraordinary results?* <br><br> **My Rating:** | I know I need better standards and habits, and I could use much more support from others. | I am learning how to get better results in life and business. I've created powerful standards, and I'm building habits to make those standards real. I've started to locate a team to help me out. | Every day I measure myself against my standards and work to ingrain good habits even deeper into my life. I have a group of experts to call upon when I need them. | I focus on raising my standards, exceeding my own expectations, and reinforcing my good habits daily. I leverage as much as I can to others who do an exceptional job in their fields, so I can do the same in mine. | I consistently produce extraordinary results in my life and business—that is the standard I live by. My good habits drive my results and success, and my *Life Team* makes what I do possible. |

How did you do? Could you see a significant difference in your numbers in the "before" and "after" audits?

My sincere hope is that you have gleaned enough from this book to help you live in mastery in every area of your life. Competition today demands more than good and even more than great—it demands mastery. I want you to live at that level in business as well as in your personal life. That's what will help you get extraordinary RESULTS Faster!

# V.I.P.s

- Document a simple list of standards to ensure actions and behaviors are directly targeted at the outcomes you desire.

- Cultures are built around standards. Many of the best opportunities happen when the people at the top have their standards documented.

- Life team members help you extend your ability to get things done, make better decisions, and do more of what you love.

- Surround yourself with *Life Team* members who have gifts and talents that complement your own and help you do life well.

- Habits, both good and bad, need to be strategically managed for anyone desiring to operate in the mastery level.

- The results we get in our lives can be directly attributed to the habits we form.

# Conclusion

So what's next?

First, let me say that this book, along with its complementary video course, has been the fulfillment of a dream for me. It's extremely rewarding to have the best of my life's work pulled together in a setting that will benefit so many people and help them live more of the life they've dreamed of. As we've been putting this work together, my hope all along the way has been that the content would be so rich that it would cause you to pause and reflect on virtually every page because of the potential wins it can make in your personal and professional life by helping you get the results you want faster.

If that's been the case in some or all of the pages, then let me conclude again with a strong recommendation that you look into our *RESULTS Faster!* course as a next step. (You can go to www.tonyjeary.com/resultsfaster to sign up for the course). In the online video course, you'll find many of my very best productivity tools, templates, and exercises in a participant's Blueprint Manual that will help you go deeper in the material we've presented, so the application will be even more impactful. It includes results maps, summary and highlight sheets, and tons of extras in addition to the hours of powerful video. You'll also get the audio to listen to on your phone or any other devise. And here's another big win for you: You'll also be given an opportunity to purchase a facilitator guide and selected updated video modules that will allow you to take the video course to your entire team. If your life has been impacted by this book, think of the multiplied ramifications of adopting my methodology inside your organization!

And of course if you'd like to discuss having me directly help you and/or your company, please e-mail me at info@tonyjeary.com. Whatever your decision, just know that the SUCCESS team and I are pulling for you to be able to live your dream life by getting the right RESULTS Faster!

# V.I.P.s by Chapter

## Chapter 1: Strategic Mindset

- Change your thinking, change your results.

- Every problem is a thinking problem, so thinking is a strategic asset.

- Ensure the principles on your *Belief Window* are true, accurate, and current—not outdated, not off mark, and not false!

- The most successful people in the world got that way because they copied the beliefs and habits of people who were more successful than they were.

- Not only balance tactical and strategic, but also be *Intentionally Strategic* about everything if you want the right results faster.

- Ask yourself this question often: *What's the best use of my time right now?* Sometimes the answer should be tactical, and sometimes it should be strategic.

## Chapter 2: Clarity

- Wealth—we all want it and it's much more than money. It's living on purpose and spending time doing what makes you happy and/or what you're truly passionate about.

- You are the architect. You can design the life you want. When you come to a crossroads in your life, you have to define with clarity what you want to have.

- Whether it's business or just you, having clearly defined values that align with your goals and vision for the future is a must.

- If you have clarity on your values, you can have a much more powerful life in terms of both your motivation and the decisions you make.

- Goals need to be written, visualized, and mentally owned. Make sure you get that, and then you can actually design your own life.

- Goals give us a blueprint or map for creating the life we envision and living by the values that are important to us.

## CHAPTER 3: FOCUS

- Know what you want more of, know what you want less of, know what you should do more of, and know what you should do less of.

- MOLO can actually be an audit of your life, per se. Finding out what you really want more of and what you want less of is an important strategic life move.

- Clearly defined HLAs are the secret to avoiding distractions and multiplying achievement, both personally and professionally.

- Activities don't count! Productivity does!

- Saying "no" smartly pays huge rewards!

- You'll have more choices to do what matters the most if you understand that you must say "no" to the things that don't matter.

## CHAPTER 4: EXECUTION

- Where and how you invest your time and energy will determine your results! Period!

- You can maximize your time by using four tools: prioritization, avoiding procrastination, organization, and delegation.

- Life truly is a series of presentations.

- Presentation/communication is more than a skillset. It's a strategic asset.

- Being strategic versus just being skillful can greatly impact the results you get.

- Life is not only a series of presentations; it's also a series of persuasions!

# Chapter 5: Force Multipliers

- Prepare, prepare, prepare!

- "What can I do to be ready?" is a powerful question we should be asking ourselves all the time.

- It really is about who you know when you want to make things happen faster.

- If you want a happier, more powerful, and more influential life; if you want to grow your career, expand your wins, and leave a legacy, then you need to be more *Intentionally Strategic* about your relationships.

- Tools work! The stronger your tool chest (arsenal), the faster you'll get results.

- Tools help you focus, they help you execute, and they provide consistency.

# Chapter 6: Leadership

- Your strategic presence or your brand has a unique impact on how people will follow your lead. Make it strong.

- Think strategically about your brand and determine how you want to be known. Then build it out and leverage it every way you can.

- Extraordinary leadership must include extraordinary influence, when it comes to getting people to take action.

- Many of the principles of persuasion have to do with helping others win. Your influence multiplies when you help others get what they want.

- There are three magic keys to building a *High-Performing Team*: accountability, communication, and trust.

- A *High-Performing Team* works together to get the very best results, and they continually reevaluate to make sure they produce the best quality.

# Chapter 7: Mastery

- Document a simple list of standards to ensure actions and behaviors are directly targeted at the outcomes you desire.

- Cultures are built around standards. Many of the best opportunities happen when the people at the top have their standards documented.

- Life team members help you extend your ability to get things done, make better decisions, and do more of what you love.

- Surround yourself with *Life Team* members who have gifts and talents that complement your own and help you do life well.

- Habits, both good and bad, need to be strategically managed for anyone desiring to operate in the mastery level.

- The results we get in our lives can be directly attributed to the habits we form.

# Glossary of Terms:

## Coined Phrases/Terms Created and Adopted by Tony Jeary

**Accelerator Matrix**: A TJI tool that includes the overall objective and generally three columns that list: 1) 5 to 10 HLAs, 2) acceleration actions related to each HLA, and 3) potential roadblocks related to each HLA to bust before they happen.

**ADOME**: An internal mnemonic for the defined type of client we want to attract and do business with: <u>A</u>ggressive and Appreciative, they want to <u>D</u>o business with TJI, <u>O</u>pen minded, <u>M</u>oney is to be made, and there is opportunity for an <u>E</u>quity play or success fee based on extraordinary results.

***Belief Window***: A model of a filter through which you view the world and make decisions accordingly. It includes everything you believe to be true, false, correct, incorrect, appropriate, inappropriate, possible, and impossible.

***Blind Spots***: Things you miss and can't even see in terms of how things are, how they work, or what's even available.

**Branding Matrix**: A tool invented by TJI to help bring clarity to either your personal brand or your organization's brand.

**Business Entertainment**: Appropriate fun factor related to and inside a presentation or meeting. Includes the use of activities, games, role-playing, and even a video clip to counter a short attention span. Usually these activities are placed at five-to-seven-minute intervals.

**Clarity**: Defined understanding of your goals and/or your vision; in essence, clearly knowing what you want to achieve.

*Elegant Solutions*: Special activities that are created when you are so clear on what you want to accomplish that multiple objectives can be simultaneously met through a single action/activity.

**Execution**: Action you take to get things done (ideally in strategic alignment with the vision).

*Favors in Advance (FIA)*: Actions to benefit others. Instead of doing favors because you expect something in return, develop an attitude of paying it forward and giving value in advance.

**Focus**: Opposite of distraction; concentrating on what really matters and filtering out what doesn't.

*Force Multiplier*: A factor (tool/activity/action) that dramatically increases (multiplies) the effectiveness of something someone is doing.

*High Leverage Activities (HLAs)*: Actions that are most relevant to your strategic agenda, success, and achievement, and that most directly impact the results you need and want. The ability to identify and focus on these significant activities is the major factor in improving and accelerating results.

*High-Performing Team (HPT)*: A team that focuses on being as effective as possible while continually reevaluating to work toward quality processes; each team member has a high level of investment in the outcome and is individually motivated.

*Intentionally Strategic*: Deliberate, planned, and intended use of overall thinking/planning.

**Leadership**: One who sets a clear vision and shares that vision with others so they can willingly focus their efforts to ensure execution of the vision with the right information, resources, and methods.

*Life Team*: A group of hand-picked individuals who help you make decisions and or execute (examples could include your executive assistant, coach, mentors, colleagues, readers, driver, lawyer, trainer, CPA, etc.).

*Low Leverage Activities (LLAs)*: The things that consume your time that have the least amount of return. They are typically task-oriented in nature and often become distractions to what your true focus should be.

**Mastery**: Performing at your top level.

**Mastery Impact Curve**: A model that demonstrates three basic levels: Good, Great, and Mastery; used to show that many stop at the Great level.

**MOLO**: A TJI tool to help an individual or organization identify what they need to eliminate so they can focus on what matters most; an evaluation of what should be done More Often and Less Often will ensure time is best invested on proactive, productive HLAs instead of on time-wasting, less effective tasks.

*People of Influence (POI)*: Those individuals who are part of your life that can and do have a huge impact on your success

*Planned Spontaneity*: Being so prepared you can respond to an audience in impromptu fashion; the better prepared you are the more spontaneity you can bring to your meetings and presentations with confidence.

**Preparation**[2]: Preparing to the extreme.

*Presentation Mastery*™: Being at the highest level of presentation effectiveness.

**Presentation Ready**: Being in a state with the right tools to respond instantly to a request for a briefing or for insight on a particular subject or area of management.

**Presentation Universe**: All the presentation opportunities in your daily life, both personal and professional (i.e., staff meetings, speeches, and one-on–ones).

*Production Before Perfection (PBP)*: A TJI principle that says you must not allow the fear of perfectionism to stop you from starting. You should most often start and perfect as you go.

**Reticular Activating System (RAS)**: A set of nerves at the bottom of the brain that acts as a gatekeeper to allow or disallow information to come into your brain, based on what you care about or need.

**Smart Reports**: A TJI term that refers to a special researched briefing on a particular subject.

**Stakeholder Matrix**: A TJI tool that facilitates great clarity regarding all those impacted and what they most care about to help insure everyone wins.

*Strategic Acceleration*: The ability to expedite change and increase effectiveness more quickly, powered by clarity, engaged with focus, and converted into superior results via execution.

*Strategic Acceleration* **Studio**: Tony Jeary's private think tank, named after his best-selling book, *Strategic Acceleration*.

**Strategic Altruism**: Being intentional about helping others short and long term.

**Strategic Goal-Setting**: Being intentional about planning for what you want to achieve (have, share, experience, give, and become).

**Strategic Health**: Being intentional about your overall well-being.

*Strategic IQ*: Intentional balance between your strategic and tactical activities.

*Strategic Mindset*: A well-thought-out set of assumptions pertaining to thinking and beliefs, as well as balancing tactical and strategic efforts.

*Strategic Parenting*: Being intentional about raising exceptional, successful children.

*Strategic Presence*: Your brand or reputation; how people perceive you personally. If you have a powerful brand (strategic presence), people are more likely to execute on your behalf. Be intentional and strategic about your brand/reputation or strategic presence.

*Strategic Procrastination*: A smart handle on both positive and negative procrastination, first introduced in Tony Jeary's best-selling book *Strategic Acceleration*.

*Strategic Selling*: Being intentional in the art of persuasion in order to get people to take action on your behalf.

*Strategic Thinking*: Another term for *Intentionally Strategic* (deliberate, planned, and intended use of overall thinking/planning).

**SWOT: An** evaluation tool for the assessment of Strengths, Weaknesses, Opportunities, and Threats.

*Targeted Polling*: Calling on specific members of the audience and asking them to share their feedback, giving the presenter the ability to tailor the presentation to more successfully impact the audience; can be done before, during a break, or during an activity.

**3D Outline™**: A powerful outline format that includes the What, Why, and How aspects of a presentation or meeting; used for shortening the planning process and to insure every minute is maximized. (Ask about TJI's 3-D Outline™ Builder Software.)

**Trust Transference**: The transfer of trust from one person's brand, reputation, and relationships to another.

**Value Arsenal**: A tool box of white papers, books, abstracts, and best practices of all kinds to help you be more valuable.

**Values Clarification**: An exercise that helps you define what matters the most to you.

*Verbal Surveying*: Asking questions of the audience during a presentation to obtain usable feedback and then adjusting accordingly (i.e., speeding up or slowing down for more or less detail).

**Vision (Results) Boarding**: A visual representation of goals and vision that motivates you to action.

# About the Author:

Tony, known as The RESULTS Guy™, is a strategist, thought leader, and prolific author of over forty titles, multiple best sellers, and hundreds of courses.

Tony is unique and sought after by the world's best. His client list has now exceeded one thousand organizations in over fifty countries. He truly is a special resource that delivers and is a "secret weapon" to many business savvy leaders.

For more than two decades, Tony has coached the world's top CEOs, entrepreneurs, and high achievers. He has personally advised the presidents of Walmart, SAM's Club, Ford, Shell, Samsung, New York Life, American Airlines, Texaco, TGI Fridays, and Firestone, as well as entrepreneurs from *Forbes* Richest 400 and even the US Senate's Sergeant of Arms.

His specialty is compressed time. He partners with selected clients to clarify their visions and ensure they stay focused so they execute with extreme accountability, resulting in carving years off most client's strategic visions. He delivers "Vision to Reality" in time frames many can't even believe.

Tony practices daily the business mantra his father taught him growing up: "Give value; do more than is expected."

Tony lives and works in DFW where, at his private RESULTS Center, he and his hand-picked team strategically assemble powerful game plans, inspire high performance, and encourage all those he touches, resulting in enhanced sales/profits, and raising companies' value.

Tony is blessed with a beautiful marriage and has three wonderful adult children, two daughters and one son-in-law who all live in Texas.

# Acknowledgments:

I want to thank all the people who have done so much to make this book a reality. Much of the credit goes to Pam Hendrickson, Jonathan Cronstedt, Travis Johnson, and the entire SUCCESS Academy team, whose invaluable contributions to the book and the *RESULTS Faster!* video course have helped us produce two masterful resources. I'm also grateful for Nonie Jobe, Tawnya Austin, Madison Walker, Morgan Collins, Boomer Mackey, Eloise Worden, Brooke Hawkins, Marlo Haft and the entire TJI team, who helped us assemble and develop the content, pulling it all together.

# What We Can Do For You

## Results Coaching

*Advice Matters*, if it's the right advice. Having coached the world's top CEOs, published over forty books and advised over one thousand clients, Tony has positioned himself with a unique track record to take serious high achievers to a whole new level of results.

## Interactive Keynotes

Tony not only energizes, entertains and educates, he also has his team work strategically and smartly with the event team to make his part as well as the entire experience a super win. An hour with Tony often changes people's lives forever and impacts an organization's results immediately. He delivers value, a fun factor, and best practices people can really use.

## Strategic Acceleration Facilitation Planning

Tony can do in a single day what takes many others days and even weeks to accomplish. He has refined a process so powerful the world travels to his private think tank (called the RESULTS Center) to experience clarity, focus, and the ability to synergistically execute. He provides at your fingertips two decades of best practices, processes, and tools for accelerating dramatic, sustained results in any organization.

## Collaborative Relationships

We selectively partner with organizations in an annual collaborative engagement where we pour into an entire organization and help build a super-charging, motivated, and engaged *High-Performing*

*Team*. We align with the C-Level management vision and become an extension of them.

See www.TonyJearyTheResultsGuy.com for five questions and answers every executive wants to know.

The bottom line is we help: CLARIFY Vision, FOCUS on What Matters Most—High Leverage Activities (HLAs)—so people EXECUTE and get the Right Results Faster!

www.tonyjeary.com

# OTHER BOOKS BY TONY JEARY:

1. Inspire Any Audience
2. Strategies for Business Peak Performance
3. Designing Your Own Life
4. Finding 100 Extra Minutes in a Day
5. Meeting Magic
6. We've Got to Stop Meeting Like This
7. Ice Breakers
8. Speaking Spice
9. A Good Sense Guide to Happiness
10. Success Acceleration
11. Happy Families
12. Fun Things to do as Kids
13. Persuade Any Audience
14. Presenting with Style
15. Building Your Dream Home
16. Too Many Emails
17. Winning Seminars
18. 136 Effective Presentation Tips
19. Complete Guide to Effective Facilitation
20. Training Others to Train
21. NLP Mastery
22. Neuro Linguistic Communication P.A.
23. 10 Essentials to Execution
24. One-On-One Presentations (Coaching)
25. Monday Morning Communications
26. Speaking from the Top
27. Nervous to Natural
28. Images of Beauty
29. Presentation Mastery for Realtors
30. Presenting Learning
31. Life Is A Series Of Presentations
32. Purpose Filled Presentations

33. Negotiation Mastery
34. The 180 Rules
35. Ultimate Health
36. Leadership 25
37. Strategic Acceleration
38. We've Got to Start Meeting and Emailing Like This
39. Thinking Pays!
40. Business Ground Rules
41. Strategic Parenting
42. Living in the Black
43. Leverage
44. Rich Relationships
45. Advice Matters
46. Strategic Selling
47. Change - Its all about Mindset
48. RESULTS Faster!

## COMING SOON:

49. Family Wealth
50. Black Card Access
51. Strategic Network Marketing
51. Money Mastery
52. Money Kit
53. Strategic Learning

# RESULTS FASTER!

The Results FASTER! digital course gives you access to the tools, skills, and techniques utilized by top companies, CEOs, and super achievers who embrace Tony Jeary's revolutionary "more results in less time" approach to goal achievement.

Following Tony's Results FASTER! success framework, you'll learn, develop, and implement actionable strategies guaranteed to keep the "results needle" in your life moving forward faster than you ever thought possible.

Join Tony for 7 weeks of video lessons as he takes you by the hand and guides you toward more of the ideas, people, and attitudes essential to your success. During your RESULTS FASTER journey, you'll develop a long-term *Results Blueprint* and measure your progress following Tony's Personalized Results Audit.

# PRODUCT OVERVIEW

### Develop an "Extraordinary Results" Mindset
- Build a solid foundation for immediate results in your personal and professional life.
- Attract more of the ideas, experiences, and people who matter into your life and career.
- Learn to positively impact others and lead them toward helping you realize success.
- Master results-oriented thinking and multiply your overall effectiveness.

### Approach Your Goals with Clarity and Focus
- Create a clear vision for your future and discover all the steps you'll take to get there.
- Learn to focus your energy on the high-leverage activities that matter.
- Use "Force Multipliers" to put more time back into your day, even as you achieve more.
- Follow your personal Results FASTER! blueprint and consistently move forward.

### Stop Waiting and Start Seeing Results
- Immediately turn your long-term dreams into achievable short-term goals.
- Astound others as you accomplish more with less by "creating time out of thin air."
- Realize what really matters to you and approach your goals with feel-good focus.
- Uncover the secret to long-term success and constant personal and professional achievement.

**VISIT FREE TONYJEARY.COM/RESULTSFASTERWEBINAR**

SUCCESS
ACADEMY